All About Venice: A Kid's Guide to the City on Water

Shah Rukh

Published by Shah Rukh, 2024.

While every precaution has been taken in the preparation of this book, the publisher assumes no responsibility for errors or omissions, or for damages resulting from the use of the information contained herein.

ALL ABOUT VENICE: A KID'S GUIDE TO THE CITY ON WATER

First edition. October 12, 2024.

Copyright © 2024 Shah Rukh.

ISBN: 979-8227558510

Written by Shah Rukh.

Table of Contents

Prologue

Welcome to Venice! Have you ever heard of a city where streets are made of water and boats glide through narrow canals instead of cars on roads? Venice, Italy, is one of the most magical and unique cities in the world. Known as the "City on Water," it has a fascinating history, beautiful architecture, and so many secrets waiting to be discovered.

In this book, you'll journey through Venice's winding canals, explore its ancient buildings, and learn about the people, stories, and traditions that make this city so special. You'll meet the gondoliers who steer their elegant boats through the water, discover why Venice has always been a hub for art and trade, and even learn how the city was built on a swampy lagoon!

Whether you dream of riding in a gondola, visiting the towering St. Mark's Basilica, or exploring the mysterious islands nearby, this book will be your guide to Venice's wonders. So, grab your explorer hat, and let's set off on an adventure through the Floating City!

Are you ready to dive into Venice's watery world? Let's go!

Chapter 1: Discovering the Floating City

Venice is one of the most magical and unique cities in the entire world! Imagine a place where there are no cars, no buses, and no trucks. Instead, Venice is a city built entirely on water. It sits on more than 100 small islands, and all these islands are connected by canals and bridges. The city doesn't float like a boat, but it looks like it does because it rises from the waters of a lagoon. That's why people often call Venice "The Floating City."

Hundreds of years ago, clever people decided to build their city in the middle of a lagoon, which is a shallow body of saltwater separated from the sea by a strip of land. But how do you build a city on water? This is where the story gets even more amazing. The people of Venice drove wooden piles, or long wooden stakes, deep into the soft ground under the water. These wooden piles act like strong legs for the city, supporting buildings and streets. Over time, these piles turned hard like stone because of the lack of oxygen underwater, and they still hold up the city today!

In Venice, instead of roads for cars, there are canals for boats. The canals are like Venice's special water roads. The biggest canal in Venice is called the Grand Canal, and it twists and turns through the city like a giant watery snake. Beautiful palaces, churches, and shops line the edges of the Grand Canal, making it one of the most famous streets—or should we say waterways—in the world. Boats of all sizes travel along the canals, taking people to work, school, and even to the store. Some people even have their own boats, just like people in other cities might have a car!

One of the most famous kinds of boats in Venice is called a gondola. Gondolas are long, sleek, and elegant. They glide smoothly through the canals, and they are driven by people called gondoliers. Gondoliers are like Venice's version of taxi drivers, but instead of driving a car, they skillfully steer their gondolas with long poles. They often wear striped shirts and hats, and sometimes they even sing songs as they row! Riding in a gondola is a peaceful and fun way to see the city.

As you glide through the canals, you'll notice that Venice is full of bridges. In fact, there are more than 400 bridges in the city! Some of the bridges are small and simple, while others are large and beautifully decorated. One of the most famous bridges is called the Rialto Bridge. It's an old stone bridge that crosses the Grand Canal, and it has shops built into it. From the top of the Rialto Bridge, you can see the boats going up and down the Grand Canal, and it's a perfect spot to take pictures.

But Venice isn't just about boats and bridges. The city is also known for its stunning architecture and history. Because Venice was once one of the richest cities in the world, it's filled with incredible buildings that were built hundreds of years ago. Some of the most famous buildings in Venice include St. Mark's Basilica, a beautiful church with golden mosaics, and the Doge's Palace, where the rulers of Venice used to live. These buildings make Venice feel like a fairy-tale city from another time.

Venice is also a city full of art and culture. It has been home to famous painters, musicians, and explorers. One of Venice's most famous explorers was Marco Polo, who traveled all the way to China and brought back amazing stories of his adventures. Venice was a place where people from all over the world came to trade goods, ideas, and culture. In fact, Venice was once one of the most powerful trading cities in Europe because it was perfectly located for ships coming from the East and the West. Merchants would bring spices, silks, and treasures to sell in Venice's markets, and the city grew rich and famous.

Walking around Venice is like stepping into the past. The streets are narrow and winding, and you never know what hidden courtyard or small bridge you might discover next. Sometimes, the streets are so narrow that two people can barely walk side by side! Many of the streets are lined with colorful houses, flower boxes in the windows, and small cafes where you can stop for a tasty snack, like gelato, which is a delicious Italian ice cream. Because there are no cars, the city is very peaceful, and all you can hear is the sound of the water gently lapping against the buildings and boats.

One of the most amazing things about Venice is that it changes with the seasons and tides. Sometimes, especially in the fall and winter, the city experiences something called "acqua alta," which means "high water." During acqua alta, the water in the canals rises so high that some of the streets and squares are flooded. The people of Venice are used to this, though. They wear tall rubber boots and put out special walkways to help people get around. After a few hours, the water goes back down, and everything returns to normal.

Venice is not just a place for tourists. Many people live there and go about their daily lives, just like in any other city. They go to school, work in shops or restaurants, and gather with friends and family. There are even some very special festivals that take place in Venice, like Carnival. During Carnival, people dress up in beautiful costumes and wear masks, and the city is filled with music, dancing, and parades. It's one of the most colorful and exciting times to be in Venice!

The food in Venice is also something special. Being a city on the water, Venice is known for its seafood. You can find fresh fish, crabs, and clams in the local markets, and there are many delicious dishes made from the catch of the day. Venice is also famous for a type of food called cicchetti, which are small snacks, kind of like tapas in Spain. You can try lots of different cicchetti, like fried meatballs, marinated vegetables, or tiny sandwiches, while exploring the city.

Because Venice is such a special and old city, people are working hard to protect it. The city is slowly sinking, and the water levels in the lagoon are rising, so there are big projects underway to help save Venice from flooding. Engineers and scientists are studying ways to protect the city so that people can enjoy its beauty and history for many more years.

In the end, Venice is like no other place on Earth. It's a city that seems to float on water, filled with boats instead of cars, and it's a place where history, art, and beauty come together. Whether you're exploring the canals on a gondola, walking across the ancient bridges, or marveling at the stunning buildings, Venice is a city that will fill you with wonder and leave you with memories to last a lifetime.

Chapter 2: The Story Behind Venice's Canals

Venice's canals are one of the most famous and fascinating features of the city, and they have a long and interesting history. Imagine walking through a city with no streets for cars, buses, or bikes—only water flowing through narrow channels lined with beautiful buildings. These watery streets are what make Venice so special. But how did they come to be? Why does Venice have canals instead of regular roads? To understand the story behind Venice's canals, we have to go back more than a thousand years.

Long ago, Venice was nothing more than a collection of marshy islands in the middle of a lagoon. The lagoon is a shallow body of water between the mainland of Italy and the Adriatic Sea. The people who first settled in this area had to be very resourceful because building a city on water is not easy! At first, the people lived in small fishing villages, and they built their homes on wooden stilts to keep them above the water. But as time went on, they wanted to create a bigger, more permanent city.

The early Venetians knew they had to find a way to build on the soft, muddy ground of the islands. So, they came up with an incredible plan. First, they hammered thousands of long wooden piles, or poles, deep into the ground. These wooden piles were made from strong trees like oak and larch. The piles went far beneath the water and the mud, reaching solid clay or sand. Once they were in place, the Venetians put large wooden platforms on top of the piles. These platforms became the foundation for the buildings and streets. What's really amazing is that the wooden piles, even after hundreds of years, are still supporting the city today!

The reason these wooden piles haven't rotted away is that they are constantly submerged in water, where there is very little oxygen.

Without oxygen, the wood doesn't decay as quickly. Over time, the water and minerals from the lagoon hardened the wood, almost turning it into stone. This is one of the reasons Venice has stood strong for so long, even though it was built in such a challenging place.

But what about the canals? Why did the Venetians decide to leave so much water between the islands instead of filling it all in with land? The answer lies in Venice's history and its location. Venice was built on a lagoon, which offered natural protection from invaders. The shallow waters and the tricky, twisting canals made it very difficult for enemy ships to reach the city. The Venetians knew that their watery streets were like a built-in defense system that kept their city safe from attack. So, they embraced the water instead of fighting against it.

The canals were not just for protection, though. They also became Venice's main way of getting around. Since there were no cars back then, people used boats to travel from one island to another. The canals became the city's transportation network, just like roads are in other cities. And because Venice was a major trading city, the canals made it easy for merchants to bring goods into the city by ship. Boats filled with spices, silk, and other treasures from faraway lands would sail right up to the merchants' doorsteps!

Over time, the Venetians became expert boat builders and navigators. They developed different types of boats for different purposes. There were large cargo boats for carrying goods, smaller boats for people to travel around, and of course, the famous gondolas. Gondolas are the sleek, elegant boats that glide through the narrow canals of Venice. They are perfectly designed for the city's tight, winding waterways. For hundreds of years, gondolas were the main way people got around Venice. Today, they are mostly used by tourists, but they remain a symbol of Venice's rich history.

One of the most important canals in Venice is the Grand Canal. The Grand Canal is like the main street of Venice, except it's made of water! It's a huge, winding canal that cuts through the heart of the city.

The Grand Canal is about two and a half miles long, and it's lined with some of Venice's most beautiful and historic buildings. Palaces, churches, and shops sit right on the water's edge, and boats of all kinds travel up and down the canal every day. The Grand Canal is so busy with water traffic that it's sometimes called Venice's "superhighway."

But the Grand Canal is just one of many canals in Venice. There are more than 150 canals in the city, and they weave their way between the islands like a web. Some of the canals are wide and open, while others are narrow and hidden away. If you explore Venice by boat or on foot, you'll discover that the canals have a charm all their own. You might find a tiny canal with colorful houses on either side, or a quiet spot where the only sound is the splash of water against the walls.

The bridges of Venice are also an important part of the story of the canals. Since the canals act like streets, people needed a way to cross from one side to the other. That's where the bridges come in. Venice has more than 400 bridges, and each one is different. Some are small and simple, while others are grand and decorated with statues and carvings. One of the most famous bridges in Venice is the Rialto Bridge. The Rialto Bridge is a huge stone bridge that crosses the Grand Canal. It has been standing for over 400 years, and it's one of the most iconic sights in Venice.

Another famous bridge is the Bridge of Sighs. This bridge has a sad story behind it. It connects the Doge's Palace, where the rulers of Venice lived, to the old prisons. Prisoners would cross the bridge on their way to jail, and it's said that they would sigh as they looked out at their last view of the city before being locked away. Even though it has a sad history, the Bridge of Sighs is one of the most beautiful bridges in Venice.

Over the centuries, the canals of Venice have played a huge role in the city's success. Because Venice is built on water, it became a powerful trading hub. Merchants from all over the world came to Venice to buy and sell goods. The canals allowed ships to sail right into the city, bringing exotic goods like spices from Asia and precious metals from Africa. Venice grew rich and powerful thanks to its canals, and it became known as "La Serenissima," or "The Most Serene," because of its wealth and beauty.

Today, the canals are still an important part of life in Venice. There are no cars in the city, so people continue to use boats to get around. There are vaporettos, which are like water buses, and water taxis that take people from one place to another. There are even special boats for collecting garbage and delivering mail! The canals are like Venice's lifeline, connecting all parts of the city and keeping everything moving.

But the canals also face challenges. Over the years, Venice has slowly been sinking into the lagoon. The rising water levels and occasional floods, known as "acqua alta," have become a serious problem for the city. During acqua alta, the canals overflow, and parts of the city are flooded with water. People wear special boots and use raised walkways to get around. The city is working on big projects to protect itself from the rising waters, but it's a constant battle to keep the canals and the city safe.

In the end, Venice's canals are more than just a way to get around—they are the heart and soul of the city. Without them, Venice wouldn't be the magical place that it is today. The canals have shaped the city's history, its culture, and its way of life. They are a reminder of the incredible ingenuity and determination of the people who built Venice on water all those years ago. So, when you visit Venice and see the shimmering canals winding through the city, you are looking at one of the most amazing achievements in the world. Venice's canals are truly a wonder, a living connection to the past, and a symbol of the city's enduring beauty and strength.

Chapter 3: Gondolas: Venice's Famous Boats

Gondolas are one of the most famous symbols of Venice, and they have been gliding through the city's canals for centuries. These sleek, black boats have become iconic, representing the charm, history, and romance of the "Floating City." Gondolas are much more than just a way to get around—they are a living connection to Venice's rich past and the craftsmanship of its boatbuilders. The story of the gondola is full of fascinating details, and it begins many hundreds of years ago, back when Venice first started becoming the bustling, water-filled city it is today.

In the early days of Venice, when the city was growing from a series of islands in the lagoon into a powerful trading hub, boats were the primary way to get around. There were no roads, only canals, and so people used various types of boats to travel, transport goods, and go about their daily lives. Over time, one type of boat, the gondola, emerged as the most popular and important vessel in the city. Gondolas were perfectly suited for Venice's narrow, winding canals, and they became the main form of transportation for people from all walks of life—merchants, nobles, and even everyday citizens used gondolas to move through the city.

In those days, there were thousands of gondolas in Venice. Each one was unique, with different designs, decorations, and colors. Gondolas were built by skilled craftsmen who worked in special boatyards called *squeri*. These craftsmen, known as *squeraroli*, passed down their knowledge from generation to generation, and they took great pride in creating boats that were not only functional but also beautiful. Some gondolas were decorated with ornate carvings and luxurious fabrics, reflecting the wealth and status of their owners. It wasn't uncommon to see gondolas painted in bright colors or covered in gold leaf to show off the owner's prestige.

The design of the gondola itself is a masterpiece of engineering. Although it may look simple at first glance, every part of a gondola has been carefully crafted to serve a purpose. One of the most interesting features of a gondola is its asymmetrical shape. If you look closely, you'll notice that one side of the boat is slightly longer than the other. This may seem strange, but there's a reason for it. Gondolas are steered by a gondolier, who stands at the back of the boat and rows with a single oar on the right-hand side. The asymmetrical shape helps the gondola glide smoothly through the water and allows the gondolier to steer the boat in a straight line, even though they're only using one oar. Without this clever design, the gondola would constantly veer off course.

Another key feature of the gondola is the *ferro*, the large metal ornament that sits on the front of the boat. The *ferro* is not just decorative; it also has symbolic meaning. The shape of the *ferro* is meant to represent the geography of Venice. The curved top of the *ferro* is like the Doge's hat (the Doge was the ruler of Venice), while the six prongs sticking out from the front symbolize the six districts, or *sestieri*, of Venice. There is even a small arch in the design that represents the Rialto Bridge, one of the most famous bridges in the city. The *ferro* also helps balance the boat and keeps it steady as it moves through the water.

While gondolas have always been important to life in Venice, their role has changed over the centuries. In the past, they were used for everything from transporting goods to carrying people around the city. Wealthy Venetians would often have their own private gondolas, much like people today have cars. These private gondolas were like floating living rooms, complete with plush seats, fine fabrics, and even small cabins to protect passengers from the weather. Some gondolas were used as water taxis, ferrying passengers from one part of the city to another.

However, as Venice grew and changed, so did the gondolas. In the 1600s, laws were passed that required all gondolas to be painted black, which is why they all look the same color today. This law was meant to curb the excessive competition among wealthy Venetians, who would try to outdo each other by decorating their gondolas in lavish styles. By making all gondolas black, the government hoped to create a more uniform and modest appearance. But even though the outside of the gondolas became more subdued, the craftsmanship and elegance of the boats themselves continued to shine through.

Over time, as new forms of transportation like steam-powered boats and motorboats were introduced, the number of gondolas in Venice began to decline. By the 20th century, gondolas were no longer the primary mode of transportation in the city. However, they did not disappear. Instead, gondolas took on a new role as a symbol of Venice's cultural heritage. Today, gondolas are mostly used for tourism. Visitors from all over the world come to Venice to take a ride in a gondola, gliding through the canals as they admire the historic buildings and soak in the atmosphere of the city.

One of the most special parts of riding in a gondola is the gondolier. Gondoliers are the skilled boatmen who row and steer the gondola using only a single oar. Becoming a gondolier is not easy—it requires years of training, practice, and even passing an exam. Gondoliers must learn how to navigate Venice's complex network of canals, how to handle the boat in all kinds of conditions, and even how to speak multiple languages to communicate with tourists from around the world. Traditionally, the role of gondolier was passed down from father to son, but today, there is an official school where aspiring gondoliers can learn the trade.

Gondoliers are known for their distinctive uniforms, which usually include a striped shirt and a straw hat with a ribbon. They also have a reputation for being great storytellers, often sharing tales of Venice's history and pointing out landmarks as they row through the canals.

Some gondoliers even sing traditional Venetian songs as they steer the boat, adding to the magical experience of gliding through the city's waterways.

Despite the fact that gondolas are now mostly used for tourism, the tradition of building gondolas by hand has been carefully preserved. There are still a few *squeri* in Venice where skilled craftsmen build and repair gondolas using techniques that have been passed down for centuries. Each gondola is made entirely by hand, and the process can take several months. The wood used to build gondolas comes from different types of trees, each chosen for its specific qualities. For example, oak is used for the frame, while larch and walnut are used for the sides and bottom. Every piece of the gondola is carefully shaped and assembled to create a boat that is both strong and graceful.

In fact, building a gondola is considered an art form. No two gondolas are exactly the same, even though they may look similar from the outside. Each gondola is a reflection of the craftsmanship and skill of the boatbuilder, and the process of creating one involves a deep understanding of both the materials and the water. The curved shape of the gondola, the angle of the oar, and even the balance of the boat are all carefully calculated to ensure that it moves smoothly through the water.

Riding in a gondola is often described as a magical experience. As the gondola glides through the narrow canals, the water reflects the sunlight and the ancient buildings rise up on either side, creating a sense of stepping back in time. Many visitors to Venice say that a gondola ride is one of the highlights of their trip, and it's easy to see why. The gentle rocking of the boat, the sound of the water lapping against the sides, and the sight of Venice's beautiful bridges and palaces make for an unforgettable experience.

One of the most romantic aspects of gondola rides is that they offer a unique view of the city. From the water, you can see parts of Venice that are hidden from view when walking on land. You might pass under a bridge where locals are chatting, or catch a glimpse of a hidden courtyard where children are playing. Gondolas allow you to experience Venice in a way that no other form of transportation can.

The tradition of gondolas is so strong in Venice that they are often used in special events and celebrations. For example, during the annual *Regata Storica*, a historical boat race that takes place on the Grand Canal, gondolas are decorated with flowers and flags as they parade through the water. Gondoliers dress in traditional costumes, and the event is a celebration of Venice's long and proud connection to its boats and waterways.

Even though gondolas are no longer used as much for daily transportation, they remain an important part of Venice's identity. The sight of a gondola gliding silently through a canal, with a gondolier standing tall at the back, is a reminder of the city's unique history and its enduring connection to the water. Gondolas are more than just boats—they are symbols of Venice's creativity, craftsmanship, and resilience.

So, the next time you see a picture of a gondola, or if you're lucky enough to visit Venice and take a ride in one, remember that you are experiencing a piece of history. Gondolas have been part of Venice's story for hundreds of years, and they continue to capture the imagination of people from all over the world. Whether used for transporting goods, carrying nobles through the canals, or giving tourists a glimpse of the city's beauty, gondolas are a testament to the ingenuity of the Venetians and their ability to thrive in a city built on water.

Chapter 4: The Secrets of St. Mark's Basilica

St. Mark's Basilica, also known as the Basilica di San Marco, is one of Venice's most breathtaking and famous landmarks. With its grand domes, glittering mosaics, and fascinating history, this magnificent church is not just a place of worship—it's a treasure trove of secrets and stories that span centuries. As you walk up to the Basilica, its beauty and intricate details can feel overwhelming. But every piece of this grand building has a story to tell, and the more you learn about it, the more you'll understand why St. Mark's Basilica is such a special place in Venice.

The story of St. Mark's Basilica begins more than a thousand years ago. Venice was a powerful and wealthy city during the Middle Ages, and its leaders wanted to build a church that would reflect its greatness. But the Basilica was not originally built where it stands today. The first church dedicated to St. Mark was constructed in 828 AD after two Venetian merchants smuggled the remains of St. Mark the Evangelist, one of the four authors of the Christian Gospels, out of Alexandria, Egypt. Legend has it that the merchants hid St. Mark's body in a barrel of pork to keep it safe from Muslim guards, who wouldn't touch the forbidden meat. The Venetians believed that having St. Mark's relics in their city would bring them protection and prestige, and they were determined to build a grand church in his honor.

However, the original church didn't last long. In 976 AD, it was burned down during a rebellion, and a new basilica was constructed in its place. This second version of St. Mark's Basilica is what you see today, although it has been added to and renovated many times over the centuries. The basilica's design is heavily influenced by Byzantine architecture, which was popular in the Eastern Roman Empire. This style is known for its large domes, elaborate mosaics, and richly decorated interiors, all of which you can see in St. Mark's Basilica.

One of the first things you'll notice about St. Mark's Basilica is its stunning façade, or front. The façade is covered in colorful marble, intricate carvings, and golden mosaics that tell stories from the Bible. If you look closely, you'll see scenes of the life of Christ, the Virgin Mary, and, of course, St. Mark himself. The mosaics on the façade have been replaced and restored many times over the years due to damage from weather and aging, but they still shine brightly, giving the basilica a sense of timeless beauty.

The most famous part of the façade is probably the four bronze horses that stand on a balcony above the main entrance. These horses are known as the Horses of St. Mark, and they have their own incredible story. They were originally part of a monument in ancient Rome and were later moved to Constantinople (modern-day Istanbul), the capital of the Byzantine Empire. In 1204, during the Fourth Crusade, Venetian soldiers captured Constantinople and brought the horses back to Venice as a symbol of their victory. For centuries, the Horses of St. Mark stood proudly on the basilica's façade, but in the 1980s, they were moved inside the basilica to protect them from pollution and weather damage. The horses you see outside today are replicas, but the originals can still be viewed inside the basilica.

Once you step inside St. Mark's Basilica, you'll be amazed by its incredible interior. The first thing that will probably catch your eye is the glittering mosaics that cover the ceilings, walls, and domes. These mosaics are made up of tiny pieces of colored glass, gold, and precious stones, and they depict scenes from the Bible and the lives of saints. In total, the mosaics cover more than 8,000 square meters, making St. Mark's Basilica one of the most richly decorated churches in the world. The golden mosaics give the interior a warm, glowing light, especially when the sunlight filters in through the windows, making the entire space feel magical.

But these mosaics are not just beautiful; they also have a deep religious meaning. The scenes depicted in the mosaics are meant to teach visitors about the Christian faith and the history of the church. For example, one of the domes shows the creation of the world, with God creating the heavens, the earth, and all living things. Another dome tells the story of Pentecost, when the Holy Spirit descended on the apostles, giving them the ability to speak in different languages so they could spread the message of Christianity. Throughout the basilica, you'll find images of angels, prophets, and saints, all carefully arranged to guide visitors through the story of salvation.

One of the most important parts of St. Mark's Basilica is the Pala d'Oro, a stunning golden altarpiece that sits behind the high altar. The Pala d'Oro is considered one of the most exquisite examples of Byzantine craftsmanship in the world. It is made of gold and covered in precious jewels, including sapphires, rubies, emeralds, and pearls. The altarpiece is decorated with intricate images of Christ, the Virgin Mary, and various saints, all surrounded by ornate patterns and designs. The Pala d'Oro was originally created in the 10th century, but it was later expanded and embellished by Venetian craftsmen over the centuries. Today, it stands as a symbol of Venice's wealth and artistic achievement.

Beneath the high altar, hidden from view, is the tomb of St. Mark. According to legend, the body of St. Mark was hidden in the basilica to protect it from thieves and invaders. For many years, the exact location of his remains was unknown, but in 1094, the body was said to have been miraculously rediscovered when a pillar in the basilica cracked open, revealing the hidden tomb. Since then, St. Mark's remains have been safely kept beneath the high altar, making the basilica one of the most important pilgrimage sites in the Christian world.

But St. Mark's Basilica holds even more secrets. Beneath the main floor of the church is a network of crypts, which were once used as burial places for important Venetian figures. The crypts are usually off-limits to the public, but during times of heavy rain or high tides, the crypts can flood, filling with water from the lagoon. This is a reminder that St. Mark's Basilica, like all of Venice, is built on water. In fact, the basilica's foundations rest on wooden piles driven into the marshy ground, just like the rest of the city's buildings. Over the centuries, the constant presence of water has taken a toll on the basilica's structure, and today, efforts are constantly being made to protect and preserve the building from flooding and water damage.

Another fascinating part of St. Mark's Basilica is the treasury, which holds an incredible collection of relics, religious artifacts, and treasures from all over the world. Many of these treasures were brought to Venice after the city's conquests, particularly after the Fourth Crusade, when the Venetians looted Constantinople. The treasury contains precious items such as gold chalices, jewel-encrusted crosses, and ancient relics believed to have belonged to saints and biblical figures. One of the most mysterious items in the treasury is a piece of cloth said to be part of the robe worn by Christ during his crucifixion. The treasury also holds a large collection of Islamic art and objects, a reflection of Venice's extensive trade relationships with the Middle East.

The bell tower, or Campanile, of St. Mark's Basilica is another iconic part of the church's history. Standing at nearly 100 meters tall, the Campanile offers a stunning view of Venice and the surrounding lagoon. However, the tower you see today is not the original. The original bell tower was built in the 9th century but collapsed in 1902 due to structural weaknesses. Miraculously, no one was hurt in the collapse, and the tower was rebuilt exactly as it had been before. Today, visitors can climb to the top of the Campanile to enjoy panoramic views of the city and the surrounding islands.

Despite its grandeur, St. Mark's Basilica is still a working church, and religious services are held there regularly. Visitors can attend mass or simply admire the beauty of the building while soaking in the sense of history and spirituality that fills the space. The basilica has witnessed many important events in Venetian history, from royal weddings to state ceremonies, and it continues to play a central role in the life of the city.

But perhaps the greatest secret of St. Mark's Basilica is the sense of wonder and awe it inspires in all who visit. Whether you are marveling at the shimmering mosaics, gazing up at the grand domes, or standing before the golden Pala d'Oro, the basilica invites you to step into a world of beauty, faith, and history. Every corner of the church holds a story, and each detail has been carefully crafted to inspire reflection and admiration. As you explore St. Mark's Basilica, you'll discover not just a building, but a living monument to Venice's rich cultural and religious heritage.

Chapter 5: Venice's Amazing Bridges

Venice is a city like no other, where the streets are canals and the cars are boats. But in a place where water separates everything, how do people get around? That's where Venice's amazing bridges come in! The city is home to hundreds of bridges, each with its own unique design and story. Without these bridges, moving through Venice would be nearly impossible for the thousands of people who live there and the millions of visitors who come to see its beauty every year. Let's take a deep dive into the world of Venice's bridges, discovering what makes them so special and how they've become such an important part of the city's identity.

First, it's important to understand why Venice has so many bridges in the first place. The city is built on a collection of over 100 small islands in the Venetian Lagoon, and all of these islands are separated by canals. These canals are like Venice's version of roads, allowing boats to travel from one place to another. But, of course, people need to walk too! So, bridges became the solution to connect the islands, allowing Venetians to cross from one side of a canal to the other easily. Over time, these bridges became an essential part of life in Venice, and they are now some of the city's most famous landmarks.

One of the most famous bridges in Venice is the Rialto Bridge, known as *Ponte di Rialto* in Italian. This bridge is not only one of the oldest in the city but also one of the most beautiful. The Rialto Bridge was originally built as a wooden bridge in the 12th century, but after it collapsed a couple of times, the Venetians decided to rebuild it in stone in the late 1500s. The stone version of the bridge is the one you can see today, with its grand arches and elegant design. The Rialto Bridge crosses the Grand Canal, which is the largest and most important canal in Venice, and it connects two of the city's main districts, San Marco and San Polo.

Walking across the Rialto Bridge is an unforgettable experience. Not only does it offer spectacular views of the Grand Canal, but it's also home to a row of small shops selling everything from jewelry to souvenirs. The bridge has become a lively marketplace where locals and tourists alike can shop while admiring the beauty of Venice. In fact, when the bridge was first built, it was designed to have shops on it because the area around the Rialto was the commercial center of Venice at the time. Today, the bridge remains one of the busiest and most popular spots in the city, making it a must-see for anyone visiting Venice.

Another bridge that holds a special place in the heart of Venice is the Bridge of Sighs, or *Ponte dei Sospiri* in Italian. The Bridge of Sighs is much smaller than the Rialto Bridge, but it's just as famous, thanks to the many stories and legends that surround it. The bridge is made of white limestone and has small windows with stone bars, giving it a very mysterious look. It connects the Doge's Palace, which was the residence of the ruler of Venice, to the city's old prison.

The Bridge of Sighs got its name because, according to legend, prisoners would sigh as they crossed the bridge, knowing that it was their last chance to see the beautiful city of Venice before being locked away in the prison. The view from the bridge's windows would have been their final glimpse of the outside world. Although it sounds sad, many people now think of the bridge as a romantic place, and it has become a popular spot for couples. There's even a saying that if two people kiss under the Bridge of Sighs at sunset while riding in a gondola, they will be granted eternal love!

But Venice's bridges aren't just for crossing the water; they are also works of art in their own right. Many of the city's bridges have been designed with incredible attention to detail, making them some of the most beautiful structures in Venice. For example, the *Ponte dell'Accademia* is one of only four bridges that cross the Grand Canal, and it's famous for its elegant wooden structure. Originally built as a temporary bridge in the 1930s, the Ponte dell'Accademia was so loved by the people of Venice that it became a permanent part of the city. From this bridge, you can enjoy one of the best views of Venice's grand palaces and the iconic dome of the Basilica di Santa Maria della Salute.

One of the most modern bridges in Venice is the *Ponte della Costituzione*, also known as the Constitution Bridge or *Ponte di Calatrava* after the architect who designed it. This bridge was completed in 2008 and is made of steel and glass, giving it a sleek and contemporary look. It connects the train station, *Stazione di Venezia Santa Lucia*, to the bus terminal at Piazzale Roma, making it an important link for people arriving in the city. Although it has a modern design, some Venetians were not happy when the bridge was first built, as they felt it didn't fit with the historic look of Venice. However, over time, the Ponte della Costituzione has become an accepted part of the city's landscape.

As you explore Venice, you'll notice that some bridges are simple and small, while others are large and grand. The smaller bridges are just as important as the bigger ones because they connect the many little islands that make up Venice. One charming example is the *Ponte dei Pugni*, or the Bridge of Fists. This small, seemingly unremarkable bridge has a rather unusual history. It was the site of fistfights between rival Venetian factions, particularly in the 17th century. These fights would take place right on the bridge, and the goal was to throw the opponent into the canal below! Today, there are no more fistfights, but you can still see four marble footprints on the bridge's surface, marking where the fighters used to stand before their matches began.

Venice is also home to a unique type of bridge called a *ponte storto*, which means "crooked bridge" in Italian. These crooked bridges don't cross the canal in a straight line like most bridges. Instead, they bend and curve in unusual ways, making them quite interesting to walk across. One example of a crooked bridge is the *Ponte Storto* near the

Church of San Felice. The bridge's unusual shape adds to the charm and mystery of Venice's winding streets and canals.

One of the things that make Venice's bridges so special is that they are pedestrian-only, meaning no cars or bikes are allowed. In fact, Venice is one of the only cities in the world where people travel mainly by foot or by boat. This gives the city a peaceful and calm atmosphere, with no honking horns or speeding vehicles. Instead, you'll hear the gentle sound of water lapping against the sides of the canals and the soft footsteps of people crossing the bridges. This slower pace of life is one of the things that makes Venice such a magical place to visit.

Venice's bridges are also important gathering places for people. Whether it's locals stopping for a quick chat or tourists pausing to take photos, the bridges are always full of life. During festivals and special events, the bridges become even more lively, with people lining up to watch parades, boat races, or fireworks displays on the canals below. One of the most famous events in Venice is the *Regata Storica*, a historic boat race that takes place every year on the Grand Canal. Crowds of people gather on the bridges to watch as beautifully decorated boats race down the canal in a celebration of Venice's maritime history.

But life on Venice's bridges isn't always easy. Because the city is built on water, the canals can flood during a phenomenon known as *acqua alta*, or "high water." When this happens, the water levels in the canals rise, sometimes spilling over onto the streets and even covering the lower parts of the bridges. During particularly bad floods, the city sets up raised walkways to help people get around without getting their feet wet. Despite the challenges posed by the flooding, the Venetians have adapted to life in their watery city, and the bridges remain a vital part of daily life.

The history and beauty of Venice's bridges continue to inspire people from all over the world. Whether you're crossing the grand Rialto Bridge, strolling across the romantic Bridge of Sighs, or exploring the hidden corners of the city via its smaller bridges, each one offers a unique perspective on Venice's rich history and culture. These bridges are not just pathways across water; they are symbols of Venice's creativity, resilience, and connection to its past.

In the end, Venice's amazing bridges are more than just structures—they are the lifeblood of the city. They connect the islands and people of Venice, making it possible to move through the city while enjoying its breathtaking views. Each bridge tells a story, whether it's a tale of ancient history, an architectural marvel, or simply a quiet place to pause and take in the magic of Venice. So, as you walk across Venice's bridges, take a moment to appreciate the beauty, history, and craftsmanship that have gone into creating these incredible structures. They are, after all, a huge part of what makes Venice one of the most enchanting cities in the world.

Chapter 6: Life in the Venetian Lagoon

Life in the Venetian Lagoon is like living in a world that's entirely different from anywhere else on Earth. Imagine a place where the land and water blend together so closely that you can't always tell where one ends and the other begins. Venice, and the lagoon it sits in, are part of a unique environment that has shaped the way people live, work, and even how animals and plants survive. The Venetian Lagoon is not just the home of Venice itself but also many smaller islands, natural marshes, and canals that make it one of the most fascinating places in the world.

First of all, what exactly is a lagoon? A lagoon is a shallow body of saltwater separated from the sea by a barrier such as a sandbar or coral reef, with small inlets allowing the water to flow in and out. The Venetian Lagoon, however, is special because it was created by a combination of both nature and human effort. Over thousands of years, rivers flowing into the Adriatic Sea deposited sediments that slowly formed the lagoon. But early Venetians played a big role too, altering the landscape to make it more livable, including building the city on wooden piles to protect it from the water. Today, the lagoon stretches over 212 square miles, making it a huge, watery playground for both nature and human life.

Living in the Venetian Lagoon is unlike living anywhere else, as daily life revolves around water. While many cities have streets filled with cars, trucks, and bicycles, in Venice and the lagoon, transportation happens mainly on boats. From small rowboats to larger motorboats, boats are the main way to get around. There are water buses called *vaporetti* that ferry people across the lagoon, taxis that zoom through the canals, and even delivery boats that bring food and goods to the markets and shops. Imagine getting a pizza delivered by boat! In Venice, this is normal, and people have adapted to this water-based way of life for centuries.

One of the most important jobs for people in the Venetian Lagoon is fishing. The lagoon is full of fish, and for generations, Venetians have relied on the lagoon's waters for their livelihood. Traditional fishermen still go out in small wooden boats, using age-old methods to catch fish, crabs, and shellfish. Some of the most famous catches from the lagoon are *moeche*, a type of soft-shell crab, and *go*, a fish that's often used in Venetian dishes. The people of Venice have a deep connection with the sea, and many of the city's famous dishes come straight from the waters of the lagoon.

But it's not just fish that make the lagoon special—it's also home to a variety of bird species. The Venetian Lagoon is a paradise for bird watchers, as it is an important stopover for migratory birds flying between Europe and Africa. Birds such as herons, flamingos, and seagulls can be spotted resting in the shallow waters or nesting on the many small islands. Some of these birds have made the lagoon their permanent home, while others only pass through during migration. Either way, the lagoon is buzzing with life, making it a great place for both nature lovers and animal enthusiasts.

The people of Venice and the surrounding islands have always found creative ways to live in harmony with the lagoon's environment. For example, the farmers on the island of Sant'Erasmo grow crops that have adapted to the salty soil. This island is often called "Venice's garden" because it provides fresh vegetables to the city's markets. Farmers grow artichokes, asparagus, and other vegetables that can survive the salty conditions of the lagoon. These vegetables are highly prized by locals, and many dishes in Venice feature fresh, seasonal produce from the islands.

The lagoon is also home to some unique traditions and cultural practices that you won't find anywhere else. One of the most famous events in Venice is the *Regata Storica*, or historic boat race, which takes place every year. This colorful event brings together Venetians of all ages, from young children to experienced rowers, to race traditional boats through the canals. Many of the boats used in the race are *gondolas* or *caorline*, a type of boat that has been used in the lagoon for centuries. The Regata Storica is not just about racing; it's a celebration of Venice's maritime heritage and a chance for people to show off their rowing skills.

But life in the Venetian Lagoon is not always easy. The city of Venice, and the lagoon itself, face challenges from rising sea levels and flooding. For centuries, Venetians have battled the waters that surround them, building barriers and systems to protect the city from high tides, known as *acqua alta*. These floods can happen several times a year, and during the worst ones, parts of Venice and the islands can be submerged under water. However, Venetians are resilient and have developed ways to cope with the flooding, such as raising walkways and using pumps to remove water from buildings. Recently, a new flood defense system called *MOSE* was built to help protect the lagoon and Venice from these rising waters, but the battle against the sea is ongoing.

One of the things that make life in the lagoon so magical is the feeling of being surrounded by history. Many of the small islands scattered throughout the lagoon are filled with ancient buildings, churches, and monasteries. One such island is Torcello, which was one of the first areas in the lagoon to be settled. Today, it's a peaceful, quiet place with a few ancient buildings that give visitors a glimpse of what life was like in the early days of the lagoon's history. Another fascinating island is Murano, famous for its glass-making tradition. For centuries, artisans on Murano have created beautiful glassworks, from colorful vases to delicate chandeliers, using techniques passed down through generations. The glass-making industry is an important part of life in the lagoon, and visitors can watch the artisans at work in their studios on the island.

Burano, another island in the lagoon, is known for its colorful houses and lace-making tradition. The brightly painted houses of Burano are one of the most iconic images of the lagoon. Each house is painted a different color, creating a vibrant rainbow effect that makes the island stand out. According to legend, the fishermen of Burano painted their houses in bright colors so that they could spot them from far out in the lagoon while fishing. Today, the island's colorful charm attracts visitors from all over the world. Burano is also famous for its handmade lace, and for centuries, the women of the island have created intricate lacework that is highly valued for its craftsmanship.

Life in the Venetian Lagoon also involves a strong connection to the past. Many of the islands were once centers of industry, where salt was harvested, and trade flourished. In fact, Venice became a powerful and wealthy city thanks to its position in the lagoon, where it controlled trade routes between Europe and the East. Ships loaded with goods like spices, silk, and precious metals would pass through the lagoon on their way to Venice, making the city one of the richest in the world during the Middle Ages and Renaissance. The lagoon's waters not only provided food and transportation but also protection from invaders. The islands and canals made it difficult for enemy ships to navigate, giving Venice a natural defense against attack.

Despite the challenges of living in a watery environment, the people of Venice and the lagoon have found ways to thrive. The lagoon is not just a place where people live; it's a living ecosystem where human life and nature are intertwined. The constant ebb and flow of the tides shape the landscape, and the people who live in the lagoon have adapted to this ever-changing environment. From the fishermen who go out each day in their boats to the artisans who create beautiful glass and lace, life in the lagoon is filled with creativity, tradition, and resilience.

In recent years, there has been a growing effort to protect the lagoon's fragile ecosystem. Pollution, overfishing, and climate change have all posed threats to the lagoon's waters and wildlife. But conservationists and local communities are working to preserve this unique environment for future generations. Projects to restore the natural marshes, reduce pollution, and manage fish stocks are helping to ensure that the lagoon remains a thriving habitat for both people and animals.

Living in the Venetian Lagoon means being constantly aware of the water that surrounds you. Whether it's the shimmering canals reflecting the sunlight or the quiet, misty mornings when the lagoon is covered in fog, the water is a constant presence. It shapes the way people move, work, and interact with their environment. The lagoon is not just a backdrop to life in Venice—it is life itself. From the bustling markets of Venice to the quiet, hidden corners of the smaller islands, the Venetian Lagoon is a place where water and land come together to create a world that is both beautiful and unique. For those lucky enough to experience it, life in the Venetian Lagoon is filled with wonder, history, and a deep connection to nature.

Chapter 7: How Venice Was Built on Water

The story of how Venice was built on water is nothing short of extraordinary. Imagine trying to build a city in the middle of a lagoon, where there is no solid ground, only mud, marshes, and water as far as the eye can see. Yet, that's exactly what the people of Venice did over a thousand years ago. Venice's story is one of human ingenuity, perseverance, and a deep connection to the water that surrounds it. It's a tale of how people found a way to make their home in one of the most challenging environments in the world and, in doing so, created a city unlike any other.

The origins of Venice go back to the 5th century, when people in the nearby region of Italy, known as the Veneto, were being attacked by invading forces, especially the Germanic tribes like the Huns and Lombards. They needed a safe place to escape from these invaders, and the Venetian Lagoon seemed like the perfect spot. The lagoon's shallow waters and many small islands provided natural protection from enemy ships. However, there was one big problem: the islands were marshy, unstable, and not suitable for building permanent homes or structures. But the early Venetians didn't let this stop them. They decided to build a city right on top of the water, using some very clever techniques.

The first challenge was how to create a solid foundation for buildings in such a watery environment. The ground in the lagoon was too soft to support the weight of buildings, so the Venetians came up with an ingenious solution: they would build on wooden piles, or poles, driven deep into the mud. These wooden piles, usually made from alder, oak, or larch trees, were driven down until they reached a layer of harder clay beneath the mud. Since wood doesn't rot when it's submerged in water and deprived of oxygen, these piles have remained strong for centuries. The waterlogged environment actually helped preserve the wood, turning the piles into a sort of stone-like material over time.

Venice's foundation was built upon millions of these wooden piles, which were driven deep into the lagoon floor. On top of the piles, the Venetians placed wooden platforms, and on top of these platforms, they laid stones. These stones created a stable base upon which they could build houses, churches, and other structures. It took an incredible amount of effort, teamwork, and resources to construct Venice this way, but the result was a city that could stand strong on its watery foundation.

But it wasn't just individual buildings that needed to be supported. The Venetians also had to figure out how to create a system of streets and canals that allowed people to move around the city. Since Venice is made up of over 100 small islands connected by canals, they needed to ensure that people could get from one place to another, either by walking or by boat. So, in addition to building on piles, the Venetians dug canals to serve as the city's streets, and they built bridges to connect the islands. These canals became the lifeblood of Venice, allowing people to transport goods, travel, and even use them as a defense against invaders.

Another key element of Venice's construction was the use of brick and stone in the buildings. Since the ground was soft and prone to shifting, the Venetians had to make their buildings as light as possible. This is why many of Venice's buildings are made of brick, which is lighter than stone. However, to make the buildings look grand and impressive, they often used stone as a covering for the brick. The most famous stone used in Venice is called Istrian stone, which comes from the Istrian Peninsula, not far from Venice. Istrian stone is strong and durable, and it's resistant to water, which made it perfect for building in Venice. You'll see it in many of the city's most famous landmarks, like St. Mark's Basilica and the Doge's Palace.

Even though Venice was built on water, the city didn't just stay in one place. Over the centuries, the Venetians actually had to shape and control the water and land around them to keep the city standing. One of the biggest challenges Venice has faced throughout its history is flooding. The waters of the lagoon rise and fall with the tides, and sometimes the city experiences what is called *acqua alta*, or "high water." During *acqua alta*, parts of the city can be completely submerged, and people have to use raised walkways or boats to get around. But the Venetians have always been resilient and inventive, finding ways to protect their city from the water that surrounds it.

In fact, the Venetians have been controlling the water around their city for centuries. In the 12th century, they began diverting rivers that flowed into the lagoon to prevent the city from silting up. If the rivers brought too much sediment into the lagoon, it could clog the canals and make the city uninhabitable. So, the Venetians carefully managed the flow of water into and out of the lagoon, creating an intricate system of canals, inlets, and barriers to protect their city. Today, Venice still faces the challenge of rising sea levels, but modern engineers have developed new ways to protect the city, including a system of floodgates called MOSE, which can be raised to block high tides from flooding the city.

But the challenges of building Venice didn't stop at the water. The city also had to contend with the weight of its buildings. Some of Venice's most famous landmarks, like St. Mark's Basilica and the Doge's Palace, are enormous structures, and their weight puts a lot of pressure on the city's fragile foundations. To make sure these buildings didn't sink into the mud, the Venetians used lightweight materials and clever architectural techniques to distribute the weight evenly. For example, the columns of St. Mark's Basilica are made of hollow bricks to reduce the overall weight of the building.

As Venice grew, so did its reputation as one of the most beautiful and unique cities in the world. By the time of the Renaissance, Venice was a major center of art, culture, and commerce, attracting visitors from all over Europe. The city's stunning architecture, its canals, and its connection to the sea made it a symbol of wealth and power. But behind all the beauty, there was always the ongoing work of maintaining the city's foundations and ensuring that Venice could stand strong in its watery home.

Venice's relationship with the water is not just a matter of practicality—it's also a source of beauty and inspiration. The canals that wind through the city are not just for transportation; they also reflect the shimmering sunlight, creating magical views that have inspired countless artists and writers over the centuries. Gondolas, with their sleek black design, have become an iconic symbol of Venice, gliding silently through the narrow canals, under bridges, and past ancient buildings. The play of light on water, the sound of the waves lapping against the stone walls, and the sight of boats gently bobbing in the canals all contribute to the unique atmosphere of Venice, a city that truly seems to float on water.

One of the most fascinating aspects of Venice's construction is how it continues to evolve even today. The city's foundations are constantly shifting, and modern engineers and architects work hard to preserve and protect the historic buildings while also making sure Venice can withstand the challenges of the future. Restoration projects are always underway, as experts carefully repair and reinforce the city's wooden piles, stone foundations, and brick buildings. Venice is a living city, and the work of maintaining it never ends.

The story of how Venice was built on water is a testament to the ingenuity, determination, and creativity of the people who founded and shaped this incredible city. From the very beginning, the Venetians have faced enormous challenges, from unstable ground to rising tides, yet they have always found ways to overcome them. Venice is a city that defies the odds, standing strong on its watery foundations for over a thousand years. It's a place where the impossible has become reality, and where the beauty of the city is inseparable from the water that surrounds it. Living in Venice means living with the constant presence of water, but it also means being part of a remarkable story of human achievement.

Chapter 8: The Masks of the Venetian Carnival

The Venetian Carnival is one of the most magical and exciting celebrations in the world, and one of the things that makes it truly special is the beautiful, mysterious, and colorful masks that people wear. These masks have been a part of Venice's history for hundreds of years, and they are more than just a fun costume. The masks of the Venetian Carnival have deep roots in the city's traditions and culture, and each mask tells a unique story. Imagine walking through the narrow streets of Venice during Carnival and seeing people everywhere in elaborate costumes, their faces hidden behind stunning masks that sparkle in the light, adding an air of mystery and enchantment to the city.

The origins of the Venetian Carnival and its famous masks date back to the Middle Ages. Venice was a city of great wealth and power at that time, and the Carnival was a way for people to celebrate before the solemn season of Lent, which is a period in the Christian calendar where people are expected to give up certain pleasures and luxuries. But the Carnival wasn't just a simple party — it was a time when the rules of society were temporarily suspended, and people were free to enjoy themselves in ways they normally couldn't. Wearing masks played a big role in this, as they allowed people to hide their true identities, which meant that everyone, rich or poor, noble or commoner, could mingle together without worrying about their social status.

In Venice, a city full of wealth, merchants, and nobility, there were strict rules about how people from different social classes should behave. But during Carnival, the masks gave people a way to escape these rules, even if just for a little while. The masks allowed for anonymity, which meant people could behave in ways they normally wouldn't — they could flirt, joke, dance, and even criticize the powerful without fear of punishment. This sense of freedom made the Carnival a time of fun, excitement, and mischief, and the masks were a key part of that experience.

One of the most fascinating things about the masks of the Venetian Carnival is that they come in many different shapes, styles, and designs, each with its own meaning and history. Some masks are simple, while others are incredibly elaborate, decorated with gold, jewels, feathers, and intricate designs. The most traditional Venetian masks are often based on characters from Italian theater, known as *commedia dell'arte*, which was a type of improvisational theater that was popular in Italy during the 16th century. In *commedia dell'arte*, each character wore a specific mask that represented a certain personality or role. For example, the character Arlecchino, or Harlequin, was a clever servant, always trying to trick his master, and his mask was usually colorful and playful.

One of the most well-known and iconic masks of the Venetian Carnival is the *Bauta*. The *Bauta* mask is unique because it covers the entire face, but it has no mouth opening. Instead, it has a sharp, jutting chin that allows the wearer to speak, eat, and drink without removing the mask. In the past, the *Bauta* was worn not only during Carnival but also at other important social events or when people wanted to keep their identity hidden. Because the *Bauta* was so effective at concealing the wearer's identity, it was often used by people who wanted to move through the city anonymously, whether for business, political intrigue, or secret meetings. The *Bauta* was usually worn with a black cloak and a tricorn hat, which added to the air of mystery.

Another popular mask is the *Moretta*, also known as the "mute mask." The *Moretta* is an oval-shaped mask made of black velvet, and it has a curious feature: it has no straps to hold it in place. Instead, the wearer holds the mask on their face by biting down on a small button inside the mask. Because of this, the person wearing the *Moretta* couldn't speak, which gave it the nickname "the mute mask." The

Moretta was especially popular among women, and its simple yet elegant design made it a favorite for ladies who wanted to add a touch of mystery to their appearance. The *Moretta* mask gave women the ability to attend social gatherings without revealing their identities, which added to the intrigue of the Carnival.

The *Volto*, or "larva," mask is another traditional Venetian mask. The *Volto* is a simple white mask that covers the entire face, giving it a ghostly, otherworldly appearance. The word "larva" in Latin means "ghost" or "mask," which is why this mask is sometimes called the ghost mask. The *Volto* was often worn with a black cloak and was one of the most common masks during Carnival because of its simplicity. The plain white mask allowed the wearer to become almost invisible in a crowd, blending in with the other masked figures moving through the city. The *Volto* has become one of the most recognizable symbols of the Venetian Carnival, and even today, you'll see many people wearing it as they parade through the streets and squares.

One of the most dramatic and eye-catching masks of the Venetian Carnival is the *Medico della Peste*, or "Plague Doctor" mask. This mask has a long, beak-like nose and was originally designed for doctors who treated patients during the Black Plague, a deadly disease that swept through Europe in the 14th century. The beak of the mask was filled with sweet-smelling herbs and flowers to protect the doctor from the bad air, which people believed carried the disease. Over time, the Plague Doctor mask became a popular part of the Carnival, symbolizing the city's history and the dangers it had overcome. Even though the mask has a somewhat eerie appearance, it is now a beloved part of the Carnival tradition, and you'll often see people dressed in full Plague Doctor costumes, with long robes and a wide-brimmed hat to match.

But the Venetian Carnival masks aren't just about hiding your identity. They are also works of art. Venetian mask makers, known as *mascherari*, are highly skilled craftsmen who have been creating these beautiful masks for centuries. The art of mask-making in Venice is a tradition that has been passed down through generations, and each mask is carefully crafted by hand. The *mascherari* use materials like paper-mâché, leather, and porcelain to create the masks, and they decorate them with gold leaf, paint, lace, and feathers. Every mask is unique, and many are inspired by the rich history, art, and architecture of Venice itself. Walking into a mask shop in Venice is like stepping into a treasure trove of color and creativity, where each mask seems to have its own personality and story.

Today, the Venetian Carnival is a time for people from all over the world to come together and celebrate the city's history and culture. During the Carnival, Venice transforms into a magical stage where everyone is invited to take part in the fun. The streets, squares, and canals fill with people in elaborate costumes, all wearing their own masks and becoming part of the grand spectacle. Music fills the air, parades wind through the city, and the atmosphere is one of celebration and joy. One of the most exciting parts of the Carnival is the contest for the best mask, where participants show off their most creative and beautiful masks in hopes of winning the grand prize.

The masks of the Venetian Carnival aren't just about fun and games, though. They represent the spirit of Venice itself: a city that has always been a little mysterious, a little daring, and always full of surprises. Just like the masks, Venice is a place where beauty and mystery go hand in hand, and where history comes alive in the most enchanting ways. The tradition of wearing masks during Carnival reminds us of Venice's unique ability to blend the old with the new, the serious with the playful, and the ordinary with the extraordinary.

For the people of Venice, wearing a mask during Carnival is more than just a tradition — it's a way of stepping into a different world, if only for a little while. Behind the mask, you can be anyone or anything you want to be. It's a time to let go of everyday worries, embrace the magic of the city, and lose yourself in the excitement and wonder of the Carnival. The masks allow people to become part of a centuries-old tradition that has been passed down through generations, and every year, the city comes alive with the colors, sounds, and secrets of the Venetian Carnival.

In the end, the masks of the Venetian Carnival are a reflection of the city itself. Just as Venice rises out of the water like a dream, with its shimmering canals and grand palaces, the masks add a layer of fantasy and magic to the Carnival. They remind us that Venice is a place where the ordinary becomes extraordinary, where the past and present come together in a celebration of life, art, and mystery. For those who visit Venice during Carnival, the masks are not just a costume — they are a key to unlocking the city's most enchanting secrets, a symbol of a world where anything is possible.

Chapter 9: The Grand Canal: Venice's Main Waterway

The Grand Canal is the most famous and important waterway in Venice, and it's often called the heart of the city. Stretching in a giant "S" shape through the center of Venice, the Grand Canal is like a big, watery road that connects many of the city's most important and beautiful places. But unlike other cities, where cars and buses drive on streets made of asphalt, in Venice, the main transportation is done by boat, and the Grand Canal is the main "road" for these boats. For centuries, this canal has been the lifeline of Venice, with everything from grand processions and festivals to everyday deliveries happening on its waters.

The Grand Canal is about 2.4 miles (3.8 kilometers) long, and at its widest point, it stretches over 300 feet (90 meters) across. As you glide along its waters, you can see some of Venice's most stunning buildings, many of which are centuries old. These buildings were built by wealthy Venetian families who wanted to show off their power and riches, and each one tells a story of Venice's glorious past. There are over 170 buildings that line the Grand Canal, and many of them are palaces, or *palazzi*, built in the Gothic, Renaissance, and Baroque styles. These grand structures reflect the city's rich history and its connections to powerful merchants, traders, and nobility.

One of the most fascinating things about the Grand Canal is that it hasn't changed much over the centuries. The buildings you see today are mostly the same ones that stood there hundreds of years ago, making it feel like you're traveling back in time when you sail down the canal. This is because Venice, being built on water, doesn't have the same room to expand as other cities. So, rather than growing outward, Venice grew upward and preserved its ancient structures. The Grand

Canal has always been the main artery of Venice, and it remains a central part of the city's life today, just as it did in the past.

To truly understand the importance of the Grand Canal, we need to go back in time to when Venice was one of the most powerful cities in the world. In the Middle Ages and the Renaissance, Venice was a major center of trade. Merchants from all over Europe, the Middle East, and Asia came to Venice to buy and sell goods like silk, spices, precious metals, and other treasures. The Grand Canal was the route they used to transport these goods to and from the city's markets. Large trading ships and merchant vessels would enter the city through the lagoon and sail down the Grand Canal, unloading their valuable cargo at the various docks and warehouses that lined its banks.

Because of its role in trade, the Grand Canal quickly became a symbol of Venice's wealth and influence. The palaces that line the canal were built by wealthy merchants and nobles who made their fortunes through trade, and they spared no expense in making their homes as impressive as possible. Many of these palaces have large, ornate facades facing the water, with beautiful arches, balconies, and marble decorations. The reason these buildings are so grand is that the wealthy families who lived there wanted to impress visitors arriving by boat. Back then, it was common for important guests, such as ambassadors, dignitaries, and merchants, to travel by boat along the Grand Canal when they came to Venice, and the grand palaces were meant to showcase the city's beauty and prosperity.

One of the most striking features of the Grand Canal is its incredible variety of architectural styles. As you glide down the canal, you can see buildings from different periods of Venice's history, each one reflecting the artistic and cultural influences of its time. For example, you'll see Gothic-style buildings with pointed arches and elaborate stonework, which were popular during the Middle Ages. You'll also see Renaissance palaces with their clean lines, balanced proportions, and large windows, which were designed to let in lots of light. And then there are the Baroque buildings, with their dramatic curves and rich decorations, which reflect the grandeur and exuberance of the 17th century. This mix of styles creates a stunning visual journey through Venice's past, and it's one of the reasons why the Grand Canal is often called the world's most beautiful street.

One of the most famous buildings on the Grand Canal is the Ca' d'Oro, or the "House of Gold." This palace is one of the best examples of Venetian Gothic architecture, and it gets its name from the gold leaf that used to cover parts of its facade. The Ca' d'Oro is known for its intricate stonework and delicate arches, and it was once the home of a wealthy merchant family. Today, it has been turned into a museum, where visitors can admire its beautiful interiors and its impressive collection of Renaissance art. As you pass by the Ca' d'Oro on the Grand Canal, it's easy to imagine what life must have been like for the powerful families who lived there, with gondolas and boats constantly arriving and departing from their private docks.

Another famous landmark on the Grand Canal is the Palazzo Ducale, or Doge's Palace. This massive, pink-and-white marble building was the home of the Doge, who was the ruler of Venice, and it served as the center of the Venetian government for centuries. The Doge's Palace is one of Venice's most iconic buildings, and its unique blend of Gothic and Renaissance architecture makes it stand out among the other palaces along the canal. The palace is connected to the famous St. Mark's Square, and it was here that many of Venice's most important political decisions were made. As you float by the Doge's Palace, you can almost picture the grand processions and ceremonies that once took place there, with the Doge himself standing on the balcony, overlooking the canal.

While the palaces and buildings along the Grand Canal are certainly impressive, the canal is also famous for its many bridges. There are four main bridges that cross the Grand Canal, and each one has its own story. The most famous of these is the Rialto Bridge, which is the oldest and most iconic of the Grand Canal's bridges. Built in the 16th century, the Rialto Bridge is a masterpiece of Renaissance engineering and design. It was originally constructed to replace a wooden bridge that had collapsed, and it quickly became one of Venice's most important landmarks. The bridge is lined with shops, and from the top, you can get a breathtaking view of the Grand Canal as it winds through the city.

Another famous bridge is the Ponte dell'Accademia, which is one of the few wooden bridges left in Venice. This bridge offers a spectacular view of the Grand Canal and the stunning Basilica di Santa Maria della Salute, a massive domed church that sits at the entrance to the canal. The Ponte dell'Accademia is a popular spot for tourists and photographers, who come to capture the beauty of the Grand Canal at sunset, when the water glows with the colors of the setting sun.

As you travel along the Grand Canal, you'll also see the Ponte degli Scalzi, a bridge that connects the Santa Lucia train station with the rest of the city. This bridge is one of the busiest in Venice, as it's the main gateway for visitors arriving by train. And finally, there's the Ponte della Costituzione, the newest of the Grand Canal's bridges. This modern, glass-and-steel bridge was built in 2008 and stands in contrast to the city's more traditional structures. It's a reminder that while Venice is a city steeped in history, it's also a place that continues to evolve and change.

The Grand Canal isn't just a scenic route for tourists; it's still a working waterway that plays an important role in the daily life of Venice. Every day, you'll see a wide variety of boats traveling up and down the canal, from gondolas carrying tourists to water taxis ferrying locals to and from work. There are also *vaporetti*, or water buses, which are the main form of public transportation in Venice. The *vaporetti* make regular stops along the Grand Canal, picking up and dropping off passengers just like a bus would in any other city. But instead of driving on roads, these buses glide along the water, giving passengers a unique perspective of the city as they travel from one place to another.

Because Venice is a city without cars, the Grand Canal also serves as a delivery route for goods. You'll often see small motorboats loaded with packages, food, and other supplies making their way down the canal, stopping at various docks to deliver their goods. Even garbage collection in Venice is done by boat! Special boats travel up and down the canal, collecting trash from homes and businesses, keeping the city clean and running smoothly.

One of the most magical experiences for visitors to Venice is taking a gondola ride along the Grand Canal. Gondolas are the traditional boats of Venice, and they have been used in the city for hundreds of years. A gondola ride along the Grand Canal gives you a chance to see the city from the water, just as Venetians have done for centuries. As you glide past the grand palaces and historic buildings, you can imagine what life was like in the days when Venice was one of the most powerful cities in the world.

The Grand Canal is also the stage for many of Venice's most important festivals and events. One of the most famous is the *Regata Storica*, or Historical Regatta, which takes place every year in September. During the regatta, the Grand Canal is filled with beautifully decorated boats, and the event includes a series of boat races that celebrate Venice's maritime history. The *Regata Storica* is one of the highlights of the Venetian calendar, and it's a chance for both locals and visitors to celebrate the city's unique relationship with the water.

In the end, the Grand Canal is much more than just a waterway; it's the lifeblood of Venice. It's a place where history, culture, and daily life come together in a way that's unlike anywhere else in the world. Whether you're admiring the grand palaces, crossing one of its famous bridges, or simply watching the boats go by, the Grand Canal offers a glimpse into the soul of Venice, a city that has been shaped by water for centuries.

Chapter 10: Rialto Market: Venice's Fresh Food Hub

The Rialto Market is one of Venice's most vibrant and lively places, filled with the hustle and bustle of daily life as locals and visitors gather to buy fresh food and experience a true slice of Venetian culture. Located near the famous Rialto Bridge, this market has been around for centuries and has long been considered the heart of Venice when it comes to fresh produce, seafood, and other delicious foods. Walking through the Rialto Market is like stepping back in time, where you can imagine how Venetians, hundreds of years ago, relied on this very spot for their daily food needs. The market's history, the sights, the smells, and the energy make it a must-see for anyone visiting Venice.

One of the most exciting parts of the Rialto Market is its fresh seafood section, known as the *Pescheria*. Venice is a city surrounded by water, so it's no surprise that seafood has always been an important part of Venetian cuisine. Every morning, fishermen bring in their daily catch from the Venetian lagoon and beyond, and the Pescheria becomes a buzzing hub of activity as sellers display their fish, shrimp, clams, octopus, squid, and more. The seafood here is as fresh as it gets, with some fish still wriggling as they're laid out on ice. The Pescheria opens early, usually around 7 AM, and closes by midday, so you have to get there early to catch the best selection. This part of the market is especially popular with local chefs and home cooks who want the finest ingredients for their dishes.

As you walk through the Pescheria, you'll notice the variety of seafood on offer. Some of the most common fish you'll find include sea bass (*branzino*), sardines, and anchovies, which are often used in traditional Venetian recipes. There's also *scampi*, a type of small lobster that is highly prized in Venice, as well as cuttlefish, which is famous for its black ink that's used to make a special type of pasta sauce. You'll also see mounds of clams and mussels, which are often served with pasta or cooked in a simple garlic and white wine sauce. If you're not familiar with all the different types of seafood, don't worry – the friendly vendors are always happy to help you choose the best fish for your needs and might even offer tips on how to cook it.

While the Pescheria is all about seafood, the other part of the Rialto Market is dedicated to fresh fruits and vegetables. This section of the market is just as lively as the Pescheria, with vendors shouting out the prices of their goods and arranging colorful displays of produce. Depending on the season, you'll find a wide variety of fruits and vegetables, many of which come from the nearby islands in the Venetian lagoon, where farmers grow everything from artichokes to pumpkins. One of the most famous vegetables grown in the region is *castraure*, which are tender baby artichokes that are a Venetian delicacy. These small, purplish artichokes are usually available in the spring, and they're often served raw in salads or lightly fried with olive oil and lemon.

During the summer months, you'll find stalls overflowing with juicy tomatoes, fresh basil, and fragrant herbs, as well as sweet, sun-ripened fruits like peaches, apricots, and melons. In the fall, pumpkins and squash take center stage, along with an array of mushrooms, including prized varieties like *porcini*, which are used in risottos and pasta dishes. The changing seasons mean that there's always something new to discover at the Rialto Market, and the vendors take pride in offering the freshest, highest-quality produce available.

In addition to the fruits, vegetables, and seafood, the Rialto Market also has stalls selling other food items like cured meats, cheeses, olives, and fresh pasta. These products are essential to Venetian cuisine, and many of the items sold at the market are made using traditional methods that have been passed down through generations. For example, you might come across *baccalà mantecato*, a creamy, whipped salt cod spread that's a Venetian specialty, or *soppressa*, a type of salami made from pork that's seasoned with garlic and spices. There are also plenty of cheeses to choose from, including local varieties like *asiago* and *montasio*, which are often served with honey or fig jam.

One of the best things about the Rialto Market is that it's not just a place to buy food – it's also a great spot to learn about Venetian culture and history. The market has been around for over 1,000 years, and it played a crucial role in Venice's rise as a major trading city. Back in the Middle Ages, Venice was one of the most powerful cities in Europe, thanks to its strategic location and its dominance of trade routes between the East and West. Merchants from all over the world came to Venice to buy and sell goods, and the Rialto area became the city's commercial hub. The market was at the center of this bustling trade, with goods like spices, silk, and precious metals arriving from as far away as Asia and Africa. Over time, the market became the go-to place for Venetians to buy not only food but also luxury items and exotic goods.

Even today, you can still feel the echoes of Venice's trading past as you wander through the market. The narrow streets around the Rialto are lined with shops selling everything from handmade pasta to Venetian glass, and the atmosphere is always lively, especially in the morning when the market is in full swing. If you're lucky, you might even hear the sound of traditional Venetian folk songs being sung by the vendors, adding to the market's unique charm.

The Rialto Market is also a great place to experience the Venetian way of life. Unlike the more touristy parts of the city, the market is still very much a place for locals, and you'll often see Venetians doing their daily shopping, chatting with the vendors, and exchanging recipes. This sense of community is one of the things that makes the Rialto Market so special. The vendors know their customers by name, and there's a real sense of connection between the people who sell the food and the people who buy it. It's not uncommon for a vendor to throw in an extra handful of tomatoes or a bunch of herbs for free, simply as a gesture of goodwill.

If you visit the Rialto Market, one of the best things to do is to pick up some fresh ingredients and have a picnic along the Grand Canal. You can buy a loaf of crusty bread, some olives, a few slices of cured meat, and a chunk of cheese, and enjoy a simple but delicious meal while watching the boats go by. There are also plenty of small cafes and wine bars near the market where you can stop for a quick snack or a glass of *ombra*, a traditional Venetian wine. Some of the cafes even offer *cicchetti*, which are small, tapas-style dishes that are perfect for sampling different flavors of Venice.

The Rialto Market isn't just a place for food, though – it's also a place for celebration. Throughout the year, there are various festivals and events that take place in and around the market. One of the most popular is the *Festa del Redentore*, which is celebrated in July. During this festival, Venetians give thanks for the end of the plague that struck the city in the 16th century. The market is decorated with colorful banners, and there are food stalls set up selling traditional dishes like *sarde in saor* (sweet and sour sardines) and fried seafood. The highlight of the festival is a spectacular fireworks display over the Grand Canal, which you can watch while enjoying a delicious meal from the market.

Another important festival is *Carnevale di Venezia*, or the Venice Carnival, which takes place in the weeks leading up to Lent. The market becomes a sea of colorful masks and costumes, and there are special stalls selling sweet treats like *frittelle*, a type of fried doughnut that's filled with cream or fruit. The market is a key part of the carnival festivities, and it's a great place to soak up the joyful atmosphere of this world-famous event.

Whether you're a foodie looking to taste the best of Venetian cuisine, a history buff interested in learning about Venice's trading past, or simply a traveler wanting to experience the authentic side of the city, the Rialto Market has something for everyone. Its combination of fresh, delicious food, lively atmosphere, and rich history makes it one of the most special places in Venice. The market has been the city's food hub for centuries, and it remains just as important to the life of Venice today as it was in the past. So, if you ever find yourself in Venice, make sure to visit the Rialto Market – it's a place where the flavors of Venice truly come to life!

Chapter 11: The Beauty of Venetian Glass

Venetian glass is one of the most famous and beautiful types of glass in the world, known for its brilliant colors, intricate designs, and incredible craftsmanship. It's a tradition that dates back centuries and has made Venice a center for artistic glassmaking. Walking through Venice, you'll see stunning glassworks in shops and galleries, from colorful vases to delicate chandeliers and even tiny, detailed glass figurines. But the true magic of Venetian glass goes far beyond just what you see on the surface – it's about the fascinating history, the careful techniques, and the stories behind every piece of glass that has been made in Venice's glass workshops.

To understand Venetian glass, you have to go back in time to when the art of glassmaking first began in the city. Glass has been made in Venice since as early as the 10th century, but it wasn't until the 13th century that it truly became famous. At that time, Venice was one of the richest and most powerful cities in Europe, known for its trade and wealth. Venetian merchants brought back valuable materials from places like Asia and the Middle East, and among these treasures were glass objects. The people of Venice quickly saw the potential in glass and began to perfect the craft, eventually becoming the best glassmakers in Europe.

One of the key moments in the history of Venetian glass was when the glassmaking workshops were moved to the island of Murano in the late 1200s. Murano, a small island just north of Venice, became the center of Venetian glassmaking for a very important reason – safety. In the old days, the furnaces used to melt glass were extremely hot and could easily cause fires. Since Venice was built mostly out of wood, the city was at risk of catching fire, so the Venetian government decided to move all the glassmaking workshops to Murano. This not only kept Venice safer but also allowed the glassmakers to focus on their craft in a dedicated space. From that point on, Murano became known around the world for its incredible glass, and it still holds that reputation today.

The glassmakers of Venice didn't just create ordinary glass objects – they invented new techniques and styles that made their work stand out from anything else. One of the most famous techniques they developed is called *millefiori*, which means "a thousand flowers" in Italian. This technique involves creating colorful patterns that look like tiny flowers or stars inside the glass. To do this, the glassmakers would combine different colors of molten glass into a single rod, then cut the rod into tiny slices, revealing the beautiful patterns inside. These slices would then be embedded into other glass objects, creating a stunning effect. Millefiori glass is still highly prized today, and you can find it in everything from beads to paperweights to vases.

Another famous Venetian glass technique is called *filigrana*, or filigree. This technique involves creating delicate patterns using thin threads of colored glass. The glassmakers would heat up the glass until it was soft and stretchy, then pull it into thin threads, which they would twist and shape into intricate designs. These threads were then fused into larger pieces of glass to create beautiful patterns that look like lace or spider webs. Filigrana glass is often used to make bowls, vases, and other decorative items, and it's admired for its light, airy quality.

Venetian glassmakers are also known for their ability to create incredibly clear glass, known as *cristallo*. In the early days of glassmaking, most glass had a greenish or cloudy tint because of impurities in the materials. But Venetian glassmakers discovered a way to remove these impurities, creating glass that was so clear it looked like crystal. This discovery made Venetian glass even more valuable, and it was used to create everything from wine glasses to mirrors. In fact, Venetian mirrors became especially famous because they were so clear and bright, and they were often framed with intricate glass decorations.

One of the most magical things about Venetian glass is its use of color. The glassmakers of Venice are experts at mixing different minerals into the glass to create brilliant, vibrant colors. For example, adding cobalt to the glass mixture creates a deep blue color, while adding gold makes the glass turn a rich red. These colors are not just painted onto the surface of the glass – they are part of the glass itself, which means they will never fade or wear away. Venetian glassmakers also developed techniques to combine different colors within the same piece of glass, creating swirling patterns, stripes, or layers of color that catch the light in mesmerizing ways. Whether it's a bright red vase, a delicate blue bowl, or a multicolored glass sculpture, the colors of Venetian glass are one of the things that make it so special.

The beauty of Venetian glass is not just in the objects themselves but also in the incredible skill and artistry that goes into making them. Glassmaking is a difficult and dangerous process that requires years of training and experience. The glassmakers, known as *maestri*, or masters, work in extremely hot conditions, with the furnaces in their workshops reaching temperatures of over 1,000 degrees Celsius. They use long metal rods to gather molten glass from the furnace, then shape it by blowing through the rod, spinning it, or rolling it on a metal table. The glass has to be shaped quickly while it's still hot and soft, and even a tiny mistake can ruin the whole piece. Once the glass is shaped, it has to be cooled very slowly in a special oven, called an *annealing* oven, to prevent it from cracking. The process is incredibly delicate, but the maestri make it look effortless.

Over the centuries, Venetian glassmakers became famous all over Europe, and their glass was considered a luxury item that only the richest people could afford. Kings, queens, and noblemen from across Europe ordered custom glassware from Venice, and owning Venetian glass became a symbol of wealth and status. Many of the most beautiful pieces of Venetian glass were made for the grand palaces and mansions of Venice itself. Chandeliers made entirely of glass, with sparkling crystals hanging from delicate arms, lit up the grand halls of Venice's wealthiest families. Mirrors framed with intricate glass flowers and leaves decorated the walls, and delicate glass goblets were used at fancy banquets. Some of these historic pieces can still be seen today in museums and historic homes throughout Venice.

One of the most exciting times to see Venetian glass is during the *Venice Carnival*, when the city comes alive with festivals, parades, and parties. During Carnival, many Venetians wear elaborate costumes and masks, and some of the masks are made from or decorated with Venetian glass. These masks often feature tiny glass beads, feathers, and other decorations that sparkle and shine in the sunlight. The glassmakers of Venice sometimes create special pieces just for Carnival, like colorful glass jewelry, glass flowers, and other fun decorations. Carnival is a time of creativity and celebration, and Venetian glass plays a big part in making the festivities even more magical.

Today, the tradition of Venetian glassmaking is still very much alive, especially on the island of Murano, where many of the world's best glassmakers continue to work. Visitors to Murano can tour the glass workshops and watch the maestri in action as they create beautiful glass objects right before their eyes. It's an amazing experience to see the glass being shaped, blown, and colored by hand, using techniques that have been passed down through generations. Some workshops even offer classes where you can try your hand at glassmaking and create your own glass masterpiece to take home as a souvenir.

Murano glass, as it's called today, is still highly prized around the world, and owning a piece of authentic Venetian glass is considered a special treasure. Whether it's a small glass bead or an elaborate chandelier, each piece of Murano glass is a work of art that reflects the beauty and history of Venice itself. Many glassmakers in Murano continue to push the boundaries of their craft, experimenting with new techniques and designs, while still honoring the traditions that made Venetian glass famous in the first place.

In a world where so many things are mass-produced, Venetian glass remains a symbol of creativity, craftsmanship, and beauty. It's a reminder of the artistry that goes into making something truly special, and of the rich history that Venice has contributed to the world. The beauty of Venetian glass is not just in its appearance, but in the story it tells – a story of a city built on water, of skilled craftsmen dedicated to their art, and of a tradition that has stood the test of time. Whether you're admiring a delicate glass vase, wearing a necklace made of colorful beads, or simply gazing at a glittering chandelier, Venetian glass has a way of capturing the imagination and reminding us of the magic that exists in the world.

Chapter 12: The Pigeons of St. Mark's Square

St. Mark's Square, or Piazza San Marco, is one of the most famous places in Venice, and if you ever visit, one of the first things you'll notice is the large number of pigeons that gather there. These pigeons have become an iconic part of the square, and many visitors love feeding them or watching them flutter around. But the pigeons of St. Mark's Square aren't just any birds – they have a fascinating history and have played a special role in Venetian life for centuries.

The story of the pigeons in St. Mark's Square goes back hundreds of years. It's believed that pigeons first became popular in Venice because of their connection to the city's rulers, the doges. The doges were the leaders of Venice, and they were incredibly powerful. They lived in the grand Doge's Palace right next to St. Mark's Square. According to legend, the doges would receive messages from other cities delivered by pigeons, known as homing pigeons. These birds were specially trained to fly long distances and return to their homes, carrying important information tied to their legs. As a result, pigeons became associated with power and communication in Venice, and they were treated with special care.

Over time, pigeons became a regular sight in St. Mark's Square. In the 19th century, it became a tradition for locals to release pigeons during important ceremonies or celebrations, especially on the day of the Ascension. The released pigeons would fly around the city and then return to St. Mark's Square, where they would be fed by the people. This tradition helped cement the pigeons' presence in the square, and they started to become a part of daily life for both Venetians and tourists.

As more and more visitors came to Venice, the pigeons of St. Mark's Square became famous in their own right. Tourists loved to feed the pigeons, and it wasn't long before street vendors started selling bags of birdseed so that people could get close to the birds. It became a popular activity for visitors to pose for photos surrounded by pigeons, sometimes with birds perched on their arms, shoulders, or even their heads! Feeding the pigeons became such a beloved tradition that many people couldn't imagine visiting St. Mark's Square without it.

The pigeons themselves became quite clever, learning that they could find plenty of food in the square thanks to the generous tourists. Over the years, their numbers grew, and St. Mark's Square became one of the most pigeon-filled places in the world. In fact, at one point, there were so many pigeons in the square that the Venetian government began to worry about their impact on the city. Pigeons are known for leaving droppings everywhere, and the sheer number of birds in St. Mark's Square was causing some problems. The pigeon droppings were damaging the beautiful historic buildings, statues, and monuments in the square, including the famous St. Mark's Basilica. The droppings can be very acidic, and over time, they can wear down the stone and marble of these precious structures, causing lasting damage.

In addition to harming the buildings, the pigeons were also starting to cause problems for the people of Venice. Large flocks of pigeons can spread diseases, and there were concerns that the birds might carry illnesses that could affect both locals and tourists. Plus, the pigeons were becoming a bit too aggressive in their search for food, sometimes bothering visitors who were trying to enjoy the sights of St. Mark's Square.

Because of these issues, the Venetian government decided to take action. In 2008, they passed a law that made it illegal to feed the pigeons in St. Mark's Square. The street vendors who used to sell birdseed were no longer allowed to do so, and tourists were encouraged to stop feeding the birds. The goal was to reduce the number of pigeons in the square and protect the city's historic buildings from further damage. While some visitors were disappointed that they could no longer feed the pigeons, many people understood the need to preserve Venice's architectural treasures.

Even though it's now illegal to feed the pigeons, they still gather in St. Mark's Square in large numbers. The birds are so accustomed to the square that they continue to flock there, hoping to find food. Tourists still love to watch them, and it's not uncommon to see children running through the square, laughing as the pigeons fly up around them. The pigeons have become a symbol of Venice in their own way, and they are as much a part of the city's identity as the canals and gondolas.

What's interesting about the pigeons is that they seem to have a special connection to St. Mark's Square. While there are pigeons all over Venice, the largest flocks are always found in the square. This could be because St. Mark's Square is one of the busiest parts of the city, with thousands of visitors passing through every day. The pigeons are drawn to the crowds, knowing that where there are people, there's often food. Even though they're not fed as much as they once were, the pigeons still find plenty of crumbs and scraps left behind by visitors, and they've learned how to survive in the heart of the city.

In fact, the pigeons of St. Mark's Square have become such a famous part of Venice that they have inspired artists, writers, and filmmakers over the years. You can find paintings of the pigeons in art galleries, and they've appeared in countless movies set in Venice. Some people see the pigeons as a symbol of freedom, flying freely through the open spaces of the square, while others view them as a reminder of Venice's long history and the many changes the city has gone through.

For the people of Venice, the pigeons are a bit of a mixed blessing. On one hand, they bring joy to visitors and add a lively atmosphere to St. Mark's Square. On the other hand, their large numbers can still cause problems, especially when it comes to keeping the square clean and protecting the historic buildings. The Venetian authorities continue to monitor the pigeon population and take steps to ensure that the birds don't cause too much damage.

Despite the challenges they pose, the pigeons of St. Mark's Square remain an enduring part of Venice's charm. For many visitors, seeing the pigeons is one of the highlights of their trip, and it's hard to imagine the square without them. Whether they're soaring above the domes of St. Mark's Basilica or waddling around the feet of tourists, the pigeons add a unique character to this already magical city.

One of the reasons the pigeons have such a strong presence in St. Mark's Square is because of the layout of the area. The square is a large, open space with few trees or other obstacles, making it the perfect place for pigeons to gather. They can fly freely from one side of the square to the other, and the wide expanse of stone gives them plenty of space to walk and search for food. The pigeons seem to enjoy the company of humans, and they're not shy about approaching people who are sitting on the benches or walking through the square.

Even though you can't feed the pigeons anymore, they're still a lot of fun to watch. Sometimes, you'll see them hopping around on the ground, pecking at crumbs or seeds. Other times, they'll take off in a flurry of wings, filling the sky with the sound of their flapping. The pigeons have a way of making St. Mark's Square feel alive, as if the square itself is buzzing with energy and movement.

If you're lucky, you might even witness one of the moments when the pigeons all fly up at once, creating a breathtaking sight. It often happens when a large group of tourists moves through the square, or when a loud noise startles the birds. For a few seconds, the sky above St. Mark's Square is filled with hundreds of pigeons, their wings glinting in the sunlight as they circle around. Then, just as quickly as they took off, they'll settle back down, returning to their spots on the ground or on the ledges of the nearby buildings.

For anyone visiting Venice, the pigeons of St. Mark's Square are a must-see. Whether you're a bird lover or just someone who enjoys the hustle and bustle of a lively city square, the pigeons add an extra layer of excitement to an already amazing place. They are a reminder that even in a city as old and historic as Venice, there is always something alive and dynamic happening. So, the next time you find yourself in St. Mark's Square, take a moment to watch the pigeons – they're part of the magic of Venice, and they have a story all their own.

Chapter 13: Exploring Venice's Hidden Alleys

Exploring Venice's hidden alleys is like stepping into a secret world that few people get to truly experience. While most tourists stick to the main streets and crowded squares, those who venture off the beaten path discover a maze of narrow passageways, quiet corners, and ancient buildings that seem to whisper stories from the past. These alleys, called "calli" in Italian, are one of the most fascinating parts of the city, full of history, mystery, and surprises at every turn.

Venice is a city unlike any other. Built on a series of islands connected by bridges and canals, it doesn't have the typical wide roads and bustling cars that most cities do. Instead, its streets are narrow and winding, often just wide enough for two people to walk side by side. These alleyways crisscross the city like a web, some leading to grand palaces and others ending in tiny courtyards that are so quiet you can hear your own footsteps echoing off the walls. Every alley has its own personality, and walking through them feels like you're exploring a living museum.

As you walk through Venice's hidden alleys, you'll notice that many of them are so narrow that you can touch both sides of the walls at once, with your arms outstretched. Some alleys are so small that they look like secret passages, barely wide enough for one person to squeeze through. Others open up suddenly into wide courtyards, where you might find a small café or a beautiful fountain surrounded by flowers. These unexpected changes in the landscape are part of what makes exploring Venice so exciting – you never know what you'll find just around the corner.

One of the best things about getting lost in Venice's alleys is discovering the beautiful old buildings that line the streets. Many of these buildings are hundreds of years old, with peeling paint, weathered bricks, and ornate windows that tell the story of a city that has stood the test of time. Some of the buildings are covered in ivy, their walls cracked with age, giving the alleys a sense of mystery and romance. As you wander through these hidden streets, it's easy to imagine what life was like in Venice centuries ago, when merchants, sailors, and nobles roamed these same paths.

The alleys of Venice often lead to hidden treasures that many visitors miss. For example, you might stumble upon a small art gallery showcasing the work of a local artist, or a tiny bookstore filled with dusty old volumes in Italian. Some alleys lead to ancient churches, where you can step inside and admire the beautiful mosaics and frescoes that decorate the walls. Others might take you to a quiet canal, where you can sit on a bench and watch the gondolas glide by, the water lapping gently against the stone.

Venice's hidden alleys are also home to some of the best local eateries and shops. While the main tourist areas are full of restaurants and souvenir stands, the small alleys are where you'll find the real gems – family-owned bakeries, cozy trattorias, and traditional craft shops. These places have been passed down through generations of Venetians, and they offer a more authentic taste of the city. You can stop for a slice of pizza, a creamy gelato, or a plate of fresh pasta, and enjoy your meal in a quiet square away from the crowds.

One of the most exciting parts of exploring Venice's hidden alleys is that you never know where you'll end up. The city is like a giant puzzle, with its streets twisting and turning in unexpected ways. Many alleys lead to bridges that cross over canals, connecting different parts of the city. Some bridges are tiny, with just a few steps, while others are large and grand, offering breathtaking views of the water below. As you cross these bridges, you can see the reflection of the colorful buildings in the canal, the gondolas floating by, and maybe even a Venetian playing a tune on an accordion.

The alleys of Venice are filled with history. As you walk through them, you're following in the footsteps of some of the most famous figures in history. Venetian merchants used these very streets to trade goods from all over the world, from silk and spices to jewels and perfumes. Artists like Titian and Tintoretto once wandered these alleys, finding inspiration in the beauty of the city. Even Marco Polo, the great explorer, grew up in Venice, and his house still stands in one of the city's narrow streets. You can almost feel the presence of these historical figures as you explore the city's hidden corners.

The alleys also have their share of ghost stories and legends. Venice is a city with a rich and mysterious past, and many of its alleys are said to be haunted by the spirits of people who lived there long ago. Some alleys are believed to be cursed, with strange events happening to those who dare to enter after dark. There are stories of ghostly figures appearing in the shadows, of lights flickering in empty buildings, and of strange sounds echoing through the streets at night. Whether you believe in ghosts or not, wandering through Venice's alleys at night can feel like stepping into another world, where the line between reality and fantasy blurs.

One of the most famous hidden alleys in Venice is the Calle Varisco, which is known for being one of the narrowest streets in the world. This tiny alley is so narrow that only one person can fit through at a time, and it feels like you're squeezing through a crack in the city itself. Calle Varisco is just one of many narrow alleys in Venice that give the city its unique character. These small, secretive streets are part of what makes Venice such a magical place to explore.

In addition to being charming, Venice's alleys are also incredibly practical. Because the city is built on water, there are no cars in Venice, so people have always relied on walking to get from place to place. The alleys allow Venetians to navigate the city quickly, and they're often used by locals who want to avoid the busy tourist areas. You might see a Venetian carrying groceries, a child playing with a ball, or an elderly couple walking hand-in-hand through the alleys, going about their daily lives. It's a reminder that, while Venice is a popular tourist destination, it's also a living city with real people who call it home.

Another fascinating aspect of Venice's alleys is the way they can change with the seasons and the tides. Venice is famous for its acqua alta, or high water, which occurs when the tides rise and flood parts of the city. During acqua alta, some of the alleys can become filled with water, turning them into temporary canals. It's a surreal sight to see water where there was once a street, and Venetians have learned to adapt to this unique aspect of life in their city. They put on their waterproof boots, roll up their pants, and continue walking through the alleys, even when the water is ankle-deep.

In the early morning, Venice's hidden alleys have a special magic. Before the city wakes up, the streets are quiet, with only the sound of the water gently lapping against the buildings and the occasional echo of footsteps in the distance. The soft light of the sunrise casts a golden glow on the walls, and the air feels fresh and cool. Walking through the alleys at this time of day feels like you have the city all to yourself, as if you've discovered a secret world that belongs only to you.

As the day goes on, the alleys become busier, with shopkeepers opening their doors, children running off to school, and tourists starting their day of sightseeing. But even during the busiest times, the alleys retain their charm and their sense of mystery. There's always a new alley to explore, a new discovery waiting just around the corner. Whether it's a hidden church, a quiet garden, or a beautiful view of the canal, Venice's alleys are full of surprises.

In the evening, as the sun sets and the city begins to quiet down, the alleys take on a different atmosphere. The shadows grow longer, and the lights from the windows cast a warm glow on the streets. It's a peaceful time to wander through the city, listening to the distant sound of music from a café or the soft murmur of voices from a nearby restaurant. The alleys feel timeless, as if they've been waiting for centuries for someone to walk through them and uncover their secrets.

Exploring Venice's hidden alleys is one of the best ways to experience the true heart of the city. While the main tourist attractions like St. Mark's Square and the Rialto Bridge are certainly worth visiting, it's in the quiet, tucked-away corners of Venice that you'll find the real magic. Each alley has its own story to tell, and every turn brings a new adventure. So, the next time you find yourself in Venice, take a detour from the crowded streets, and lose yourself in the winding alleys of this beautiful, mysterious city. You never know what you might discover.

Chapter 14: The History of Venice's Trade Empire

The history of Venice's trade empire is one of the most fascinating stories in the history of Europe and the Mediterranean world. It all began with a small group of islands in the Venetian Lagoon, where the early settlers of Venice started to build their homes. These settlers were mostly refugees fleeing from invasions on the mainland, but their strategic position on the water would soon transform Venice into one of the greatest trading powers the world had ever seen. Over time, Venice developed into a city that was known not just for its beauty and art, but also for its wealth, its power, and its dominance over trade routes that connected Europe with the East.

The rise of Venice as a major trade empire can be traced back to its unique location. Situated on the edge of the Adriatic Sea, Venice was perfectly positioned to control the flow of goods between the East and the West. The city's early settlers recognized the value of their location and began to build a thriving economy based on trade. Because Venice was surrounded by water, it had to rely on ships to move goods in and out of the city, and from the very beginning, Venetians became expert shipbuilders and sailors. Their ability to navigate the seas would become one of the keys to their success.

Venetians were some of the most skilled merchants in the world, and they quickly learned how to trade with other regions in Europe and beyond. One of the main reasons Venice was so successful in trade was because it formed alliances with powerful kingdoms and empires. The Venetians understood the importance of diplomacy and often negotiated deals that allowed them access to valuable markets. In particular, Venice established strong ties with the Byzantine Empire, which was one of the most powerful empires of the time. This relationship gave Venice a foothold in the Eastern Mediterranean, and it allowed the city to become the gateway for luxury goods like silk, spices, and precious metals from the East.

As Venetian merchants sailed to places like Constantinople, Alexandria, and other major cities of the Eastern Mediterranean, they brought back goods that were highly prized in Europe. Spices like pepper, cinnamon, and cloves were extremely valuable because they were rare and hard to come by in Europe. Silk, which came from China, was another luxury item that Venetian merchants traded in large quantities. These goods were sold in Venice's bustling markets, and they made the city incredibly wealthy. Venetian traders were also known for dealing in other goods such as glass, wool, textiles, and grain. The wealth generated from this trade was so immense that Venice became one of the richest cities in the world.

One of the turning points in the history of Venice's trade empire came during the Crusades. The Crusades were a series of military campaigns launched by European powers to reclaim the Holy Land from Muslim control. Venice played a crucial role in these campaigns, not by fighting, but by providing the ships and resources that the Crusaders needed to travel to the Middle East. In return for their assistance, Venice was granted special trading privileges in the cities that were captured by the Crusaders. This allowed Venetian merchants to expand their reach even further, and they became the dominant trading power in the Eastern Mediterranean.

One of the most famous examples of Venice's involvement in the Crusades was the Fourth Crusade. In 1202, a group of Crusaders approached Venice to ask for ships to carry them to the Holy Land. The Venetians agreed, but when the Crusaders were unable to pay for the ships, the Venetians offered them a deal: they would transport the Crusaders if they helped capture the city of Zara, a rival trading city on the Adriatic Sea. The Crusaders agreed, and Venice gained control of Zara. But the story doesn't end there. The Crusaders went on to attack Constantinople, the capital of the Byzantine Empire, and after they captured the city, Venice gained enormous wealth and new territories in the process.

The capture of Constantinople marked the height of Venice's trade empire. The city had now become one of the most important powers in the Mediterranean, controlling key trade routes and colonies across the region. Venice's colonies stretched from the coast of the Adriatic Sea to the islands of Crete and Cyprus, and even parts of Greece. These colonies served as important hubs for Venetian trade, and they helped to secure the city's dominance over the flow of goods between Europe and the East.

The wealth that flowed into Venice from trade allowed the city to grow and prosper in ways that few other cities could. The Doge's Palace, the Basilica of St. Mark, and many of Venice's other famous buildings were constructed during this time, funded by the profits from trade. Venetian merchants built grand palaces along the Grand Canal, and the city became known for its art, culture, and architecture. Venice's rich and powerful families, many of whom made their fortunes through trade, also became patrons of the arts, commissioning works from some of the greatest artists of the time, including Titian, Tintoretto, and Veronese.

Venice's trade empire wasn't just about luxury goods. The city was also a major player in the shipbuilding industry, and its shipyards, known as the Arsenal, were some of the largest and most advanced in the world. The Venetian Arsenal was a massive complex where thousands of workers built ships for Venice's merchant fleet and navy. Venice's control over the seas depended on its ability to maintain a strong and powerful navy, and the Arsenal allowed the city to build ships quickly and efficiently. At its peak, the Arsenal could produce a fully outfitted ship in just a matter of days, thanks to its assembly-line style of production.

While Venice's trade empire brought great wealth and power to the city, it also faced many challenges. One of the biggest threats to

Venice's dominance came from other emerging powers, particularly Portugal and Spain. In the 15th century, Portuguese explorers began to discover new sea routes to the East by sailing around Africa. This was a major blow to Venice because it allowed European merchants to bypass the Venetian-controlled trade routes in the Mediterranean. Suddenly, goods like spices and silk could be imported directly from Asia, without having to pass through Venetian hands. This shift in trade routes marked the beginning of the decline of Venice's trade empire.

Another challenge that Venice faced was the rise of the Ottoman Empire. The Ottomans, who were based in modern-day Turkey, gradually expanded their control over the Eastern Mediterranean, capturing many of the territories that had once been under Venetian control. The fall of Constantinople to the Ottomans in 1453 was a major turning point, as it cut off Venice from many of its traditional trading partners in the East. Despite these challenges, Venice remained a major trading power for many years, but its dominance over Mediterranean trade was never quite the same.

Venice's decline as a trade empire was gradual, but by the 17th century, the city had lost much of its influence. However, the legacy of Venice's trade empire can still be seen today. The city's grand palaces, churches, and bridges are all reminders of the immense wealth and power that Venice once wielded. Venetian glass, which became famous during the height of the city's trade empire, is still made on the island of Murano, and Venice's cultural heritage continues to attract visitors from around the world.

The history of Venice's trade empire is a story of ingenuity, ambition, and resilience. From its humble beginnings as a small settlement on the water, Venice rose to become one of the most powerful and wealthy cities in the world, thanks to its strategic location, its skilled merchants, and its mastery of the seas. Although Venice's trade empire eventually declined, the city's impact on global trade and culture is still felt today. Venice's ability to adapt to changing circumstances, its diplomatic skills, and its innovative spirit made it one of the most extraordinary cities in history. The story of Venice's trade empire is a testament to the city's enduring importance and its remarkable place in the history of the world.

Chapter 15: The Tall Towers of Venice

The tall towers of Venice are one of the city's most iconic and fascinating features. These soaring structures, known as campaniles, rise above the rooftops and are scattered throughout Venice. While many visitors to Venice are familiar with the famous bell tower in St. Mark's Square, the city is actually home to dozens of these tall towers, each with its own unique story, history, and significance. These towers not only served important functions in Venice's past, but they also offer a glimpse into the architectural and engineering marvels that helped shape the city. Over the centuries, they have become symbols of Venice's resilience, creativity, and grandeur, and they continue to draw the attention of people from around the world.

The most famous of all the towers in Venice is undoubtedly the Campanile di San Marco, or St. Mark's Bell Tower. Standing at nearly 99 meters (325 feet) tall, this majestic tower dominates the skyline of Venice. The original bell tower was built in the 9th century, but over the years, it underwent numerous renovations and reconstructions. The version of the tower that we see today was completed in 1514, and for centuries, it served as both a watchtower and a lighthouse for sailors navigating the Venetian Lagoon. From the top of the Campanile di San Marco, guards could watch for approaching ships, look out for fires in the city, and sound the alarm in case of danger. It was also used as a signal tower, where the ringing of bells would announce important events, such as the arrival of the doge or the beginning of a festival. The tower is topped with a golden statue of the archangel Gabriel, who watches over the city from his lofty perch.

However, the Campanile di San Marco has not always stood as it does today. In 1902, after standing tall for centuries, the tower collapsed without warning. Fortunately, no one was hurt, but the loss of this beloved symbol of Venice was a great blow to the city. The people of Venice immediately began planning to rebuild the tower, and within 10 years, the Campanile was reconstructed to its original form, using many of the same materials. Today, visitors can take an elevator to the top of the tower and enjoy breathtaking views of Venice and the surrounding islands. On a clear day, it's even possible to see as far as the distant Dolomite Mountains.

But St. Mark's Bell Tower is just one of many tall towers in Venice. Each neighborhood, or "sestiere," in Venice has its own campanile, and each tower tells a different story about the city's history and culture. One of the oldest and most unique towers in Venice is the leaning Campanile of San Giorgio dei Greci. This tower belongs to a Greek Orthodox church, and it leans noticeably to one side, making it one of Venice's most curious landmarks. The reason for its tilt is the soft, marshy ground on which it was built. Like many structures in Venice, the campanile was constructed on wooden piles driven deep into the mud, but over time, the ground shifted, causing the tower to lean. Despite its precarious angle, the Campanile of San Giorgio dei Greci has stood for centuries, and it remains an important symbol of Venice's Greek community.

Another famous leaning tower in Venice is the Campanile of Santo Stefano. Located near the Rialto Bridge, this campanile also leans to one side, giving it the nickname "the leaning tower of Venice." The tower's tilt is even more pronounced than that of San Giorgio dei Greci, and it's one of the most photographed landmarks in the city. The Campanile of Santo Stefano was built in the 13th century, and like many of Venice's towers, it served as both a bell tower and a watchtower. Today, its leaning silhouette is a reminder of the challenges that come with building a city on water.

One of the tallest and most elegant campaniles in Venice is the tower of San Giorgio Maggiore, located on the island of San Giorgio just across the water from St. Mark's Square. The church and its campanile were designed by the famous Renaissance architect Andrea Palladio, and the tower is one of the best examples of classical architecture in Venice. The white marble façade of the church and the towering campanile create a striking contrast against the blue waters of the lagoon. Visitors can take an elevator to the top of the campanile, where they are treated to panoramic views of Venice, the lagoon, and the surrounding islands. The island of San Giorgio Maggiore is often quieter than the busy streets of central Venice, making it a peaceful spot to escape the crowds and enjoy the beauty of the city from above.

One of the most mysterious and lesser-known towers in Venice is the Campanile of San Francesco della Vigna. This tall, slender tower rises above a quiet neighborhood in the Castello district, far from the main tourist attractions of Venice. The campanile is unique for its simple and elegant design, which was inspired by the architecture of ancient Rome. Like many of Venice's campaniles, it has a fascinating history. According to local legend, the site where the tower now stands was once a vineyard owned by St. Mark, the patron saint of Venice. It's said that when St. Mark visited Venice, he had a vision of an angel who told him that this land would one day become a great city. In honor of this prophecy, the Venetians built a church and campanile on the site, and the vineyard was named San Francesco della Vigna.

The bells of Venice's campaniles have long played an important role in the life of the city. In the past, the ringing of the bells was used to mark the passing of the hours, to announce the start of religious services, and to signal important events. Each bell tower in Venice had its own unique set of bells, and each bell produced a different sound. The people of Venice could tell which bell was ringing just by listening to the tone, and they knew whether it was announcing a festival, a fire, or the arrival of a dignitary. Even today, the bells of Venice continue to ring out across the city, filling the air with their melodic tones and adding to the charm of this magical place.

The construction of Venice's campaniles was no easy task. Building tall towers on the unstable ground of the Venetian Lagoon required great skill and ingenuity. The Venetians developed advanced engineering techniques to ensure that their towers would remain standing, despite the shifting sands and rising waters of the lagoon. One of the most important innovations was the use of wooden piles, which were driven deep into the mud to create a stable foundation. These piles, made from water-resistant wood like oak and larch, were packed tightly together to form a solid base for the tower. Over time, the wood became petrified, turning as hard as stone and ensuring the stability of the tower.

However, even with these advanced techniques, not all of Venice's towers have survived the test of time. Many campaniles have been damaged or destroyed by fires, floods, or earthquakes, and some have had to be rebuilt multiple times. Despite these challenges, Venice's campaniles have stood tall for centuries, serving as symbols of the city's strength and resilience. Today, they are some of the most beloved landmarks in Venice, and they continue to inspire awe and admiration in all who visit.

In addition to their historical and architectural significance, Venice's campaniles also offer some of the best views of the city. From the top of these towers, visitors can see the maze of canals, the red-tiled rooftops, and the shimmering waters of the lagoon stretching out in all directions. The view from the top of a campanile is like no other, and it provides a unique perspective on the beauty and complexity of Venice. Whether you're standing atop the Campanile di San Marco, gazing out from the tower of San Giorgio Maggiore, or admiring the leaning campaniles of San Giorgio dei Greci and Santo Stefano, the experience of climbing a Venetian bell tower is one that will stay with you for a lifetime.

The tall towers of Venice are more than just architectural wonders – they are symbols of the city's rich history, its resilience in the face of adversity, and its deep connection to the sea. These towers have witnessed centuries of change, from the rise and fall of Venice's trade empire to the challenges of modern-day life in a city built on water.

As you walk through the narrow streets of Venice, you can't help but look up at these towering structures and feel a sense of awe at the ingenuity and determination of the people who built them. Whether you're exploring the famous Campanile di San Marco or discovering one of the lesser-known towers hidden in Venice's quieter neighborhoods, the tall towers of Venice are sure to leave a lasting impression.

Chapter 16: Venice's Unique Festivals

Venice is a city known for its incredible beauty, history, and unique festivals that attract people from all over the world. Throughout the year, Venice hosts a variety of celebrations, each with its own special traditions, costumes, and events. These festivals are deeply rooted in Venetian culture and history, and they have been celebrated for centuries. They are a way for Venetians to honor their past, showcase their creativity, and bring people together in joyful celebration. From the extravagant Carnival of Venice to the serene Festa del Redentore, these festivals make Venice come alive with music, art, and excitement.

One of the most famous and iconic festivals in Venice is the Carnival of Venice (Carnevale di Venezia). Held every year in the weeks leading up to Lent, Carnival is a time when Venetians and visitors alike dress in elaborate costumes and wear beautifully decorated masks. The tradition of wearing masks during Carnival dates back to the 12th century when Venetians would disguise themselves to allow people of all social classes to mingle freely without being recognized. This created a sense of mystery and equality, as people could interact without revealing their true identities.

The costumes worn during Carnival are often inspired by the styles of the 18th century, with flowing gowns, ornate hats, and luxurious fabrics. The masks, which are perhaps the most famous symbol of Venice's Carnival, come in all shapes and sizes. Some masks cover only the eyes, while others cover the entire face. They are decorated with gold, silver, feathers, and jewels, and each mask is a work of art in itself. During Carnival, the streets, squares, and canals of Venice are filled with people in these dazzling costumes, creating a magical atmosphere unlike anything else in the world.

One of the highlights of Carnival is the Flight of the Angel (Volo dell'Angelo), a spectacular event that takes place in St. Mark's Square. During this tradition, a performer dressed as an angel descends from the top of the Campanile (St. Mark's Bell Tower) on a cable, flying over the square and waving to the crowd below. The angel is usually someone who won a competition during the previous year's Carnival, and the event marks the official opening of the festivities. Thousands of people gather in the square to watch the Flight of the Angel, and it's a moment filled with excitement and anticipation.

Another important tradition during Carnival is the Best Mask Contest, where participants can compete to see who has the most beautiful or creative mask. People from all over the world come to Venice to take part in this contest, and the competition is fierce! Judges look at the craftsmanship, originality, and beauty of each mask, and the winners are announced at the end of the festival. The contest is a celebration of Venice's rich artistic heritage and the creativity of its people.

While Carnival is perhaps the most famous of Venice's festivals, it is by no means the only one. Another important festival in the city's calendar is the Festa del Redentore (Feast of the Redeemer), which takes place in July. This festival has a much more solemn and religious origin than Carnival. It dates back to 1576 when Venice was struck by a devastating outbreak of the plague. At the height of the epidemic, the Venetian Senate vowed to build a church dedicated to Christ the Redeemer (Il Redentore) if the plague would end. When the plague finally subsided, the magnificent Church of the Redeemer was built on the island of Giudecca.

Every year, Venetians celebrate the Festa del Redentore to give thanks for the end of the plague. The highlight of the festival is a special procession across a temporary floating bridge that is built over the Giudecca Canal, connecting Venice to the Church of the Redeemer. Thousands of Venetians and visitors walk across this bridge to attend a solemn religious service at the church. The procession is a deeply spiritual event that reflects the city's gratitude for its survival during a time of great suffering.

But the Festa del Redentore is not all solemnity and reflection. After the religious service, the festival becomes a joyful celebration, with fireworks lighting up the sky over the lagoon. Venetians take to their boats, which are decorated with colorful lanterns and flowers, and gather in the waters around St. Mark's Basin to watch the spectacular display. The fireworks last for over an hour, and they are accompanied by music and cheers from the crowds. For many Venetians, the Festa del Redentore is one of the most important and beloved events of the year, a time to come together with family and friends to celebrate life and give thanks.

Another unique festival in Venice is the Regata Storica (Historical Regatta), which takes place every September. The Regata Storica is a thrilling boat race that celebrates Venice's maritime heritage and the city's centuries-old tradition of rowing. The event begins with a grand parade of historical boats, known as the Corteo Storico, which sails along the Grand Canal. The boats are decorated with bright colors, and the rowers wear traditional 16th-century costumes, creating a scene that looks like something out of a Renaissance painting.

After the parade, the regatta itself begins. The boat races are divided into different categories, with men, women, and even children competing in various types of traditional Venetian boats, including the iconic gondolas. The most prestigious race is the Gondolini Regatta, where the best rowers in Venice compete in small, lightweight gondolas called gondolini. The race is fast and intense, with rowers powering their boats through the narrow canals and under the city's bridges. Thousands of spectators line the banks of the Grand Canal to cheer on the competitors, and the atmosphere is electric.

Venice's festivals are not limited to these well-known events. There are many other smaller festivals that take place throughout the year, each with its own special charm. One such festival is the Festa della Sensa (Feast of the Ascension), which commemorates Venice's historical relationship with the sea. During the Festa della Sensa, a grand ceremony known as the Wedding of the Sea takes place, where the Mayor of Venice throws a gold ring into the waters of the Adriatic Sea to symbolize the city's eternal bond with the sea. This tradition dates back to the year 1000 and is a reminder of Venice's maritime power and the importance of the sea in the city's history.

Another interesting festival is the Festa di San Martino, which is celebrated in November. This festival honors St. Martin of Tours, a beloved saint in Venice, and is especially fun for children. During the Festa di San Martino, children dress up in costumes and go door-to-door singing songs and asking for sweets, much like Halloween in other parts of the world. Traditional Venetian pastries, such as a special cake shaped like St. Martin on horseback, are made for the occasion, and families gather to share meals and celebrate together.

In addition to these traditional festivals, Venice is also home to several modern cultural events that have gained international recognition. The Venice Biennale, for example, is a prestigious art exhibition that takes place every two years. Artists from all over the world come to Venice to showcase their work, and the city becomes a hub of creativity and innovation during the event. The Venice Biennale has expanded over the years to include festivals dedicated to architecture, film, and music, making it one of the most important cultural events in the world.

The Venice Film Festival, which is part of the Biennale, is the oldest film festival in the world, dating back to 1932. Held every year in late August or early September, the Venice Film Festival is a glamorous event that attracts some of the biggest names in cinema. Film stars, directors, and producers walk the red carpet at the Lido, Venice's famous beach resort, while movie lovers flock to the city to see the latest films and catch a glimpse of their favorite celebrities.

Whether you're attending a centuries-old tradition like Carnival or experiencing the cutting-edge art of the Biennale, Venice's festivals offer something for everyone. They are a celebration of the city's rich history, its artistic spirit, and its enduring connection to the sea. Venice's festivals bring people together, both Venetians and visitors, to share in the joy, beauty, and magic of this extraordinary city. Through these celebrations, Venice's past comes alive, and the city's unique culture continues to thrive in the present.

Chapter 17: Murano: The Island of Glassmakers

Murano is one of the most fascinating islands near Venice, famous around the world for its incredible glassmaking tradition. This small island, located just a short boat ride away from Venice, has a rich history and a deep connection to the art of glassblowing that goes back more than a thousand years. People travel from all over the world to visit Murano and witness firsthand how its talented artisans create beautiful, intricate glass pieces that seem almost magical. Murano glass is known for its unique beauty, vibrant colors, and delicate designs, and the island itself is filled with history, culture, and creativity.

The story of Murano's glassmaking began in the year 1291 when the Venetian government ordered all the glassmakers in Venice to move their workshops to Murano. At that time, Venice was a city of wooden buildings, and the furnaces used by glassmakers posed a serious fire hazard. To protect the city, the decision was made to relocate all glass production to Murano. This move not only made Murano the center of glassmaking, but it also helped preserve the secrets of the craft. The techniques used by Murano's glassmakers were considered highly valuable, and the Venetian authorities made sure these methods stayed within the island. In fact, glassmakers who tried to leave Murano and take their skills elsewhere could face severe punishment!

Because of this, Murano became the only place in the world where certain glassmaking techniques were practiced, and it grew into a powerful and prosperous community. The glassmakers were so respected that they enjoyed special privileges, like being allowed to marry into noble Venetian families. Over the centuries, they perfected their craft, passing down their skills from generation to generation, and turning Murano glass into a symbol of luxury and artistry.

What makes Murano glass so special is not just the centuries of tradition behind it, but also the extraordinary craftsmanship involved in creating each piece. Glassmaking is an art that requires incredible precision, skill, and creativity. The process starts with the melting of different types of sand, which are heated in a furnace at extremely high temperatures until they turn into liquid glass. The glassmakers then use long metal rods to shape the molten glass, blowing air into it or using tools to mold it into different forms.

The most famous technique used by Murano's glassmakers is called glassblowing. This technique involves blowing air into a molten ball of glass to create hollow shapes like vases, bowls, or bottles. It may sound simple, but it takes years of practice to master. The glass must be kept at just the right temperature, and the glassmaker has to work quickly because the glass cools and hardens very fast. As they blow and shape the glass, the artisans spin the rod, stretch the glass, and sometimes add colors or decorations. Watching a glassblower at work is truly mesmerizing—one moment, they're working with a glowing blob of molten glass, and in the next moment, it transforms into a beautiful, delicate object.

One of the things that makes Murano glass so famous is the use of vibrant, striking colors. Murano's glassmakers developed special techniques to create glass in a wide range of colors by adding different minerals to the molten glass. For example, adding copper creates a green color, while cobalt turns the glass a rich blue. Gold and silver can be added to create glittering effects, and sometimes, glassmakers layer colors to create intricate patterns or swirls. The use of color in Murano glass is often bold and dramatic, making each piece a true work of art.

But it's not just glassblowing that made Murano famous. Over the years, the island's artisans developed many other techniques to create stunning glass pieces. One of these techniques is millefiori, which means "a thousand flowers" in Italian. This method involves creating small, colorful patterns that look like tiny flowers within the glass.

Millefiori pieces are made by layering different colors of glass and then slicing the glass into thin pieces, which are then embedded into larger objects like bowls, plates, or jewelry. The result is a beautiful, intricate pattern that looks like it's filled with tiny blossoms.

Another famous technique is filigree glass (or latticino), which involves creating delicate, lacy patterns inside the glass. This technique requires an extraordinary amount of skill, as the glassmaker has to pull thin threads of glass and arrange them into patterns, all while working with hot, molten glass. The filigree patterns can be spirals, stripes, or intricate grids, and they are often combined with colorful glass to create stunning effects. Filigree glass is highly prized for its beauty and the precision required to make it.

Murano's glassmakers are also known for their ability to create glass sculptures, which are incredibly detailed and often resemble animals, flowers, or abstract shapes. These sculptures are made by shaping glass while it's still hot and pliable, using a combination of tools and hand movements to mold the glass into complex forms. The glass can be twisted, stretched, and layered to create textures and details, making each sculpture unique. Some glassmakers even specialize in making tiny, delicate glass animals, like birds, horses, or dolphins, which are popular souvenirs for visitors to the island.

As you walk through the narrow streets of Murano, you'll notice that the island is filled with glass shops and studios, each showcasing the incredible variety of glass art created here. From large chandeliers that sparkle in the sunlight to tiny glass beads used in jewelry, the range of glass objects on display is truly amazing. Many visitors take the opportunity to watch glassblowers at work in their studios, where they can see the entire process of creating glass objects, from the melting of the glass to the final shaping and decorating.

One of the most iconic types of glass produced in Murano is Venetian glass chandeliers. These chandeliers are known for their elegance and grandeur, often featuring intricate designs with many arms, flowers, and decorations made entirely of glass. They are a perfect example of how Murano's glassmakers combine artistry and craftsmanship to create pieces that are both functional and beautiful. Venetian chandeliers have adorned palaces, theaters, and homes around the world, and they continue to be a symbol of luxury and refinement.

Murano's glassmaking tradition is so important that the island even has its own museum dedicated to the craft. The Museo del Vetro (Glass Museum) in Murano is home to a vast collection of glass objects, from ancient Roman glass to modern masterpieces created by contemporary artists. Visitors can explore the history of glassmaking, learn about the different techniques used by Murano's artisans, and admire the incredible skill and creativity that goes into each piece of glass. The museum also holds exhibitions that showcase the work of famous glassmakers and artists, making it a must-visit destination for anyone interested in the art of glass.

Today, Murano's glassmakers continue to innovate and push the boundaries of their craft. While they honor the traditions passed down through the centuries, they also experiment with new techniques, materials, and designs. Some glassmakers work with international artists to create modern, avant-garde glass art, while others focus on preserving the classic styles that have made Murano glass famous. This blend of tradition and innovation is what keeps Murano's glassmaking industry alive and thriving, even in the face of competition from mass-produced glass items made in other parts of the world.

Despite the challenges of modern times, Murano remains a magical place where glass is not just a material, but a medium for expressing beauty, creativity, and artistry. The island's glassmakers are not only craftsmen but also artists who continue to inspire and amaze people with their skill and imagination. Whether you're admiring a delicate glass sculpture, watching a glassblower create a vase before your eyes, or purchasing a piece of Murano glass to take home as a souvenir, the magic of Murano's glass is something you'll never forget.

In the end, visiting Murano is not just about seeing beautiful glass objects; it's about experiencing a centuries-old tradition that has shaped the identity of this small island and its people. It's about understanding the hard work, dedication, and passion that go into every piece of Murano glass, and about appreciating the incredible artistry that continues to make Murano a world-renowned center of glassmaking.

Chapter 18: The Magic of Venice at Night

Venice is a city like no other, full of winding canals, ancient buildings, and charming bridges. But while Venice is beautiful during the day, something truly magical happens when the sun sets, and the city transforms under the cloak of night. The hustle and bustle of the day give way to a quiet, mysterious atmosphere as the city's streets and canals glow softly in the moonlight. The night air in Venice feels different—more peaceful, more enchanting—and for anyone lucky enough to wander through its hidden alleys, across its bridges, or along the shimmering canals, it feels like stepping into a dream.

As the sun dips below the horizon, the light reflecting off Venice's canals shifts from the golden hues of the day to a silvery shimmer. The famous Grand Canal, usually filled with boats and vaporettos, becomes calmer. Gondolas glide slowly through the still water, their passengers enjoying the quiet and romance of the evening. The lights from the palaces lining the canal reflect off the water like twinkling stars, creating a magical mirror of the city itself. It's easy to imagine that nothing has changed for centuries, as the grandeur of Venice's past feels alive in every ripple of the canal.

One of the most enchanting places to visit in Venice at night is St. Mark's Square. During the day, this square is packed with tourists, but after dark, it transforms into a serene, almost mystical space. The majestic St. Mark's Basilica and the towering Campanile glow softly in the light of the surrounding lamps. The intricate details of the basilica's mosaics and statues seem even more impressive under the gentle glow of the night, and the square itself feels almost like a grand stage set for a romantic drama. Musicians play soft melodies in the background, filling the air with the sound of violins and pianos. Couples stroll hand in hand, and a sense of calm hangs over the square, making it a perfect place to sit and take in the beauty of Venice after dark.

Walking through the narrow alleys of Venice at night feels like exploring a secret world. The winding streets, often quiet and deserted, are lined with ancient buildings whose stone walls seem to whisper stories from centuries past. With fewer people around, it's easier to notice the small details—the old iron lanterns that cast flickering shadows on the walls, the soft sound of water lapping against the canal walls, or the echo of footsteps in the distance. Each corner you turn feels like an adventure, and it's easy to get lost, but in Venice, getting lost at night only adds to the magic.

The bridges of Venice, which are beautiful during the day, become even more magical at night. Crossing the Rialto Bridge after dark is an unforgettable experience. This iconic bridge, one of Venice's most famous landmarks, offers stunning views of the Grand Canal. At night, the canal is lit by the lights from the buildings and boats, creating a scene that feels like it belongs in a fairy tale. The shops lining the bridge are often closed, which means fewer people and more space to enjoy the peaceful view of the city's glittering waterways. Each bridge you cross in Venice at night feels like a gateway to another world, and it's hard not to be captivated by the quiet beauty all around.

For many visitors, one of the most romantic experiences in Venice is taking a gondola ride at night. During the day, gondola rides are popular with tourists, but at night, they feel much more intimate and special. As you drift along the canals in a gondola, the only sounds you hear are the soft splash of the oar in the water and the occasional murmur of conversation from the city's hidden corners. The gondolier may even serenade you with a traditional Venetian song, adding to the enchantment of the evening. Floating through the quiet canals, past ancient palaces and under stone bridges, it feels as though you've stepped back in time. The stillness of the night amplifies the beauty of Venice, making it a truly unforgettable experience.

In addition to its canals and bridges, Venice's hidden courtyards and piazzas also come alive at night. Tucked away from the main tourist areas, these small squares often feel like secret gardens. Surrounded by old buildings with ivy-covered walls, and illuminated by the warm glow of lanterns, these courtyards offer a peaceful retreat from the busier parts of the city. Sitting in one of these quiet corners, you can hear the distant sounds of the city—a gondola passing by, the gentle hum of a boat's engine, or the soft chatter of people enjoying an evening walk. These hidden spots offer a glimpse of the everyday life of Venetians, and at night, they are especially charming.

One of the most beautiful aspects of Venice at night is the play of light and shadow across the city. The narrow streets and canals are often dimly lit by old-fashioned lanterns, creating long, mysterious shadows on the walls and water. The effect is both haunting and beautiful, as the shadows seem to dance with the movement of the water. The buildings, with their tall windows and balconies, take on a ghostly appearance in the moonlight, and the entire city feels like a living painting. It's easy to see why Venice has inspired so many artists, writers, and poets over the centuries—there's something about the city's night-time beauty that sparks the imagination.

Venice is also known for its vibrant nightlife, though it's quite different from the noisy, bustling nightlife of other cities. Instead of clubs and bars, Venice offers a more relaxed, elegant experience. Many people enjoy sitting in an outdoor café, sipping a glass of wine or a cappuccino, and watching the world go by. In some areas, you can find live music performances or street artists entertaining small crowds. These performances often take place in charming squares or along the water, where the sound of the music mingles with the soft lapping of the canals. Whether it's a jazz band, a classical string quartet, or a traditional Italian singer, the music adds to the enchantment of Venice at night.

If you're lucky enough to visit Venice during one of its many festivals, the city's nighttime magic becomes even more spectacular. During events like the Venetian Carnival or the Festa del Redentore, the city is filled with lights, decorations, and celebrations. In the evening, you might see people wearing elaborate masks and costumes, adding an air of mystery to the city. Fireworks light up the sky, reflecting off the canals and creating a dazzling display of color and light. The entire city seems to come alive with excitement, and the nighttime celebrations continue late into the evening, making Venice feel even more magical and festive.

For those who want a different perspective on Venice at night, climbing one of the city's tall towers, like the Campanile of St. Mark's or the Torre dell'Orologio, offers breathtaking views. From above, the city looks like a sparkling jewel, with the canals winding like silver ribbons through the streets. The rooftops of the old buildings glow in the moonlight, and you can see the outlines of the islands in the distance. The view from these towers at night is truly awe-inspiring, and it gives you a sense of how timeless and magnificent Venice really is.

Ultimately, what makes Venice so magical at night is the way the city invites you to slow down and appreciate its quiet beauty. With fewer crowds and the peaceful stillness of the canals, you can take your time exploring the city's hidden corners, soaking in the history, the architecture, and the romance. Every alleyway, every bridge, and every reflection in the water feels like a piece of a larger story—one that has been unfolding for centuries. Venice at night is not just a place to visit; it's an experience that stays with you long after you've left, like a beautiful dream you don't want to wake from.

Whether you're strolling through St. Mark's Square, gliding down the Grand Canal, or simply sitting by the water and watching the city's lights twinkle, the magic of Venice at night is unforgettable. It's a city that reveals its true charm and mystery after the sun goes down, making it a place of endless wonder and enchantment.

Chapter 19: Venice's Famous Art and Paintings

Venice is not just famous for its canals, gondolas, and stunning architecture; it's also a city with a deep and fascinating history when it comes to art and paintings. For centuries, Venice has been home to some of the world's most celebrated artists, and the city itself has been a great source of inspiration for painters from all over the globe. Walking through Venice is like walking through an open-air museum. Almost everywhere you look, there's art—whether it's the breathtaking frescoes on the ceilings of churches, the elaborate mosaics that adorn ancient buildings, or the priceless paintings hanging in galleries. Venice's artistic history is one of the richest in the world, and its masterpieces have had a huge impact on the development of European art.

One of the most important things to know about Venetian art is that it developed its own unique style over time, separate from the art movements happening in other parts of Italy, like Florence or Rome. While cities like Florence focused on perfect proportions and classical themes during the Renaissance, Venice embraced color, light, and emotion in a way that was different from anywhere else. Venetian artists were known for their vibrant use of color, the way they played with light and shadows, and their ability to create a feeling of depth and movement in their paintings. This gave Venetian art a magical, almost dreamlike quality that made it stand out.

One of the most famous Venetian painters of all time is Titian. Born in the late 1400s, Titian became one of the greatest painters of the Renaissance, and his works are still admired today. Titian was known for his incredible use of color, which made his paintings feel alive. He was a master at creating rich, deep reds, glowing oranges, and golden yellows, which gave his works a sense of warmth and vibrancy. He painted everything from religious scenes to portraits of important people, and his ability to capture the human figure in such realistic and dynamic ways made him a favorite among the wealthy and powerful. His paintings can be seen in many places around Venice, and his influence on the art world was enormous. He inspired countless artists, and his work marked a turning point in how color was used in paintings.

Another giant of Venetian art is Tintoretto, who was known for his dramatic, almost theatrical style of painting. Tintoretto's paintings often feel like they are bursting with energy. He loved to paint scenes that showed intense action, with figures that seem to leap off the canvas. His use of light and shadow helped him create paintings that are filled with drama and emotion. One of his most famous works is "The Last Supper," which you can find in the Church of San Giorgio Maggiore in Venice. In this version of the famous biblical scene, the painting feels full of motion and tension, with bright light streaming in from above and figures moving in all directions. Tintoretto's bold style and powerful compositions made him one of the most important figures in Venetian art, and his works can still be found in churches and galleries all around the city.

Veronese is another Venetian artist who made a lasting mark on the art world. Known for his grand, detailed, and colorful paintings, Veronese was a master at creating large-scale works that told complex stories. His paintings are filled with beautiful details—elaborate costumes, intricate patterns, and impressive architecture—that draw the viewer in. One of his most famous works is "The Wedding at Cana," which depicts a huge banquet scene filled with people, food, and decorations. This painting is a perfect example of how Venetian artists loved to celebrate color, detail, and the richness of life. Veronese's works were known for their grandeur and beauty, and they can be found in many places in Venice, including the Doge's Palace and St. Mark's Basilica.

Of course, Venice itself is often the subject of great art. Many painters, both Venetian and foreign, have been inspired by the city's unique beauty—the shimmering canals, the way the sunlight reflects off the water, the old palazzos with their crumbling stone facades, and the famous skyline with its domes and bell towers. One of the most famous foreign artists who captured the beauty of Venice is Canaletto. Canaletto was known for his detailed, almost photographic paintings of Venice. He painted scenes of the Grand Canal, the bustling squares, and the stunning architecture with such precision that you can almost feel like you're standing in the city yourself when you look at one of his works. Canaletto's paintings became extremely popular, especially among wealthy travelers who wanted to take a piece of Venice back home with them. His works were like postcards from Venice, showing all the sights and scenes that made the city so enchanting.

Another foreign artist deeply inspired by Venice was J.M.W. Turner, an English painter known for his use of light and atmosphere. Turner visited Venice several times, and he fell in love with the city's ethereal beauty. His paintings of Venice are not as detailed as Canaletto's, but they capture the mood and feeling of the city in a magical way. Turner was fascinated by the way the light changed in Venice—the way the mist rolled over the canals in the early morning, or how the sunset made the water glow like liquid gold. His paintings of Venice feel almost dreamlike, with soft colors and blurred lines that make the city seem like it's floating in a haze of light and water. Turner's love for Venice helped him create some of his most beautiful works, and his ability to capture the city's magical atmosphere has inspired many artists who came after him.

Beyond the paintings found in museums and galleries, Venice itself is a work of art, and this can especially be seen in its incredible churches. Venice is home to many churches that are filled with beautiful frescoes, mosaics, and altarpieces. One of the most famous is St. Mark's Basilica, which is covered in glittering mosaics that tell stories from the Bible. These mosaics, made from thousands of tiny pieces of glass, are masterpieces in their own right and show the incredible skill of Venetian artists. Walking into St. Mark's Basilica feels like stepping into a treasure chest, with gold and color everywhere you look. Other churches, like the Church of the Frari and the Church of San Sebastiano, are also filled with beautiful paintings, sculptures, and decorations, showing how deeply connected Venice's religious life is to its art.

Another fascinating aspect of Venetian art is the tradition of sculpture. Venice is home to some truly remarkable sculptures, both inside its churches and out in public spaces. One of the most famous sculptures in Venice is the Bronze Horses of St. Mark's, a set of four life-sized horse statues that stand on the balcony of St. Mark's Basilica. These horses are incredibly old and have a fascinating history—they were originally made in ancient Greece, then taken to Rome, then Constantinople, and finally brought to Venice in the 13th century. The horses are a symbol of Venice's power and wealth, and they have become an iconic part of the city's art and architecture.

Venice's art history is also closely tied to its festivals, especially the Venetian Carnival. During Carnival, people wear elaborate masks and costumes, turning the entire city into a living work of art. These masks, which are often decorated with gold, feathers, and jewels, are inspired by Venice's long tradition of theater and performance art. Many of the masks are handmade by skilled artisans, and each one is a unique piece of art. The Venetian Carnival is a celebration of creativity, beauty, and imagination, and it's a perfect example of how deeply art is woven into the fabric of Venice's culture.

In addition to its famous painters and sculptors, Venice has also been home to many important art schools and workshops. The Accademia di Belle Arti in Venice is one of the oldest and most prestigious art schools in Italy, and it has trained generations of artists who have gone on to become famous around the world. Venice's workshops, especially those on the island of Murano, are also famous for their art, particularly their glassmaking. Murano glass is known for its beauty, craftsmanship, and vibrant colors, and it is considered a form of art in its own right. Many glassmakers in Venice create stunning glass sculptures, vases, and chandeliers that are sold all over the world, and visiting a glass workshop on Murano is like watching an artist at work.

In conclusion, the art and paintings of Venice are an essential part of the city's soul. From the masterpieces of Titian, Tintoretto, and Veronese to the stunning mosaics of St. Mark's Basilica, art is everywhere in Venice. Whether it's the grand paintings that tell stories of Venice's history and religion, or the small details like a fresco on a ceiling or a sculpture in a square, Venice is a city that celebrates beauty, creativity, and artistic expression at every turn. It's no wonder that artists from all over the world have been drawn to Venice for centuries, and its legacy as one of the greatest art cities in the world continues to this day. Venice's art is not just something to admire—it's something that stays with you, long after you leave the city, as a reminder of the incredible creativity and beauty that human beings are capable of.

Chapter 20: Exploring the Islands Around Venice

Exploring the islands around Venice is like stepping into a whole new world each time you hop on a boat. While Venice itself is known as the "Floating City," it's just one part of a much larger lagoon filled with many fascinating islands, each with its own unique history, culture, and charm. These islands are like hidden gems waiting to be discovered, and they offer a chance to see different sides of Venetian life and history that you might not experience in the main city. From the glassmakers of Murano to the colorful houses of Burano, there's always something exciting and unexpected to see as you explore the islands around Venice.

One of the most famous islands near Venice is Murano, and it's known all over the world for its glassmaking. Murano is just a short boat ride from Venice, but it feels like entering a place with its own magical charm. For hundreds of years, the glassmakers of Murano have been creating beautiful works of art from glass. This tradition goes back to the 13th century, when the Venetian government decided to move all the glassmakers to Murano to keep their techniques secret and to prevent fires in the main city (since glassmaking involves a lot of heat and flames). Walking through Murano, you'll see shops filled with delicate glass sculptures, colorful vases, and sparkling chandeliers, all made by hand. You can even visit glassmaking workshops and watch the artisans at work. It's fascinating to see them shaping molten glass into intricate designs with just a few tools and a lot of skill. Murano glass is famous for its vibrant colors, and the way the light shines through the glass makes everything feel even more magical. Many visitors like to take home a piece of Murano glass as a special souvenir, but even if you don't buy anything, the experience of seeing the glassmaking process up close is unforgettable.

Another island that's definitely worth exploring is Burano, which is known for its brightly colored houses and its tradition of lace-making. As soon as you arrive on Burano, you'll notice that every house is painted in a different color—some are bright blue, others are orange, pink, or yellow. The story goes that fishermen used to paint their houses in bold colors so they could find their way home in the thick fog that sometimes blankets the lagoon. Walking through the narrow streets of Burano feels like stepping into a fairytale, with the colorful houses reflected in the canals that wind through the island. Burano is also famous for its lace-making, a craft that has been passed down through generations. The women of Burano used to spend hours creating delicate lace by hand, and Burano lace was once highly prized by the wealthy and royal families of Europe. Today, you can visit the Museum of Lace to learn more about this tradition and see some of the finest examples of lacework ever made. You can also watch artisans create lace in the shops, using the same techniques that have been used for centuries. It's amazing to see how much detail goes into each piece of lace, and it's a reminder of the rich history of craftsmanship that exists on these islands.

Not far from Burano is the island of Torcello, which is one of the oldest settlements in the Venetian lagoon. In fact, before Venice itself became a powerful city, Torcello was the center of life in the lagoon. Today, Torcello is much quieter, with only a handful of people living there, but it's a beautiful and peaceful place to visit. One of the most important sites on Torcello is the Basilica di Santa Maria Assunta, which dates back to the 7th century. Inside the basilica, you'll find stunning mosaics that are over a thousand years old, including a massive mosaic of the Last Judgment that covers an entire wall. These mosaics are considered some of the finest examples of Byzantine art in Italy, and they give you a sense of how important Torcello once was. As you walk around the island, you'll notice that it feels very different from the busy streets of Venice or the colorful houses of Burano. Torcello is quiet, with wide open spaces, fields of wildflowers, and ancient ruins that hint at its long and storied past. It's the perfect place to relax and imagine what life must have been like in the lagoon centuries ago.

Another fascinating island to visit is San Michele, which is Venice's cemetery island. San Michele might not sound like the most exciting place to visit, but it has a special, peaceful beauty that makes it worth exploring. The cemetery on San Michele is where many famous Venetians, including artists, musicians, and poets, are buried. The island is surrounded by tall, brick walls, and as you walk through the rows of gravestones, you'll notice how quiet and serene it feels. There are also beautiful cypress trees lining the paths, giving the island a sense of calm and reflection. San Michele is an important part of Venice's history, and visiting the island offers a moment to pause and appreciate the lives of the people who helped shape the city. You can even visit the graves of famous people, like the composer Igor Stravinsky and the poet Ezra Pound, who found their final resting place on this peaceful island.

If you're looking for a more off-the-beaten-path experience, Sant'Erasmo is another island that's definitely worth visiting. Sant'Erasmo is known as the "vegetable garden" of Venice because it's where much of the fresh produce that's sold in the markets of Venice is grown. The island is mostly rural, with fields of artichokes, tomatoes, and other vegetables stretching out into the distance. It's a great place to rent a bike and explore the countryside, as there are quiet roads and beautiful views of the lagoon. The pace of life on Sant'Erasmo is slower than in Venice, and it's a wonderful place to get a sense of what life is like outside the busy tourist areas. You can also visit the Torre Massimiliana, a 19th-century fortress on the island that was built to protect Venice from invaders. Climbing to the top of the tower offers stunning views of the lagoon and the surrounding islands, and it's a great spot for taking photos or just enjoying the scenery.

There's also the island of Lido, which is very different from the other islands in the lagoon. Lido is famous for its beaches, and it's the perfect place to go if you want to take a break from sightseeing and relax by the sea. The beaches of Lido are sandy, which is unusual for Venice, and they stretch for miles along the coast. Lido is also home to the Venice Film Festival, one of the most famous film festivals in the world. Every year, movie stars and directors from all over the globe come to Lido to premiere their films, and the island becomes a hub of excitement and glamour. If you're lucky enough to visit during the film festival, you might even spot a celebrity or two walking along the streets. Lido is also known for its grand hotels, like the famous Hotel Excelsior, which has hosted many famous guests over the years.

Another island that's worth exploring is Giudecca, which is just across the canal from Venice. Giudecca is a quieter, more residential island, but it has a lot to offer visitors. One of the most famous landmarks on Giudecca is the Church of the Redeemer (Chiesa del Redentore), which was built in the 16th century as a thank-you offering after the city was saved from a terrible plague. The church is one of Venice's most important religious sites, and every year in July, a special festival is held to celebrate the end of the plague. During the festival, a temporary bridge is built across the water to connect Venice and Giudecca, and people walk across it in a grand procession. Giudecca is also known for its beautiful gardens and quiet streets, making it a great place to take a relaxing stroll away from the hustle and bustle of Venice.

Each of these islands has its own unique character and charm, and exploring them gives you a deeper understanding of the rich history and culture of the Venetian lagoon. Whether you're marveling at the glass creations on Murano, wandering through the colorful streets of Burano, or soaking up the peaceful atmosphere of Torcello, each island offers something different and special. The islands around Venice are like hidden treasures, each with its own stories to tell, and they are an essential part of the Venetian experience. By taking the time to explore these islands, you'll discover the incredible diversity and beauty that exists just beyond the main city, and you'll come away with a deeper appreciation for the magical world of the Venetian lagoon.

Epilogue

And so, our adventure through Venice comes to an end, but the magic of this city on water will stay with you forever. We've traveled through its narrow canals, marveled at its grand buildings, and learned about the people and traditions that make Venice so unique. From the graceful gondolas to the sparkling glass of Murano, Venice is truly a city like no other.

Even though our journey in this book is over, Venice has many more stories to tell. Whether you visit in person one day or imagine it through the pages of books, Venice will always be a place of wonder and discovery. The city may be built on water, but its history and beauty are as strong as stone.

So, next time you hear about Venice, you'll know just how special it is—a city where the past flows with the present, and every corner holds a new secret. Who knows? Maybe one day, you'll sail down the Grand Canal yourself and see the magic of Venice up close.

Until then, keep exploring, keep learning, and remember that there's always more to discover in this amazing world. Venice will be waiting!

The End.

www.ingramcontent.com/pod-product-compliance
Lightning Source LLC
Chambersburg PA
CBHW061352160726

47995CB00001B/275